DEDICATION

To my adored magical black cat Puma, for your devotion and unwavering love.

CONTENTS

Dedication	1
Introduction	3
Spell Casters	4
The Moon Phases	6
The Planets	10
The Angels	12
The Chakras	15
The Stones	18
The Trees	22
The Herbs	24
The Oils	27
The Candles	29
The Tarot Cards	31
The Elements	35
The Animal Presence	39
Creating Your Altar	40
White Magic Spells	42
Black Magic Spells	112
Epilogue	144

INTRODUCTION

White and Black magic spells have been cast since time began, as ancient as the world itself from the serpent in the tree of life. Spell casting offers us access to higher powers to push your desires into reality. Spell casting gives us the power to control the forces that may affect us. White magic spells can be cast to attract money, cure illness, and bring fourth lovers, and business partners. Black spells can be cast to control others, hex enemies, silence enemies, against law enforcement, win in court, and create pacts. Spells are more commonly used to attract good luck, for love, marriage proposals, new business and games of chance.

White and black magic allow you to manifest your desires quickly using all available elements to your benefit. By being aware of the properties of the elements, moon phases and the effect it has on people and the planet, you can start to use it to your full advantage. Each element holds its own particular power ready to bestow upon you its' power remember, you can use them interchangeably. Potent spell casting comes from acquired knowledge, passed down through generations for those new to spell casting an openness to expand your current level of ability. This book will be your springboard to broaden your intuition assisting you to intuitively add personalized elements suited for you and your personal set of intentions. As you progress in casting spells your power will grow allowing you to manifest quicker each time. White and Black magic like any other endeavor involves practice, the more spells you perform the more effective and precise your spells will become.

NOTE: Spells should not take the place of your physician. Spells are not recommended for treating serious illness. Spells can be used in collaboration of your Doctors advice. Spells are powerful lore passed on from generations. When casting black magic, make sure it is the path you wish to take and that the spell is appropriate for your intentions. Protect yourself when invoking spirits, clearly state whom you wish to summon. Use spells with caution.

SPELLCASTERS

Clarity of intention is crucial in obtaining favorable results. Absorb all knowledge presented in these chapters before attempting any spells, as each chapter builds upon itself leading you to casting powerful potent spells. In dealing with white magic remember that the most important element is and always will be, love. Having positive thoughts along with favorable expectations during spell casting hold a magic all there own.

The spells within this book use the elements listed interchangeably. If at anytime you are unable to find an element for the desired spell, you can improvise by drawing the element in parchment paper or substituting an element with another ingredient that comes to mind. As your intuition grows alternative elements will come quickly to mind to use in these situation. So don't fret if you are missing an element.

Spell casters should focus on moon phases, as they are extremely powerful aspect in spell casting. The lunar phases affect our minds, body and the planet itself. As a novice spell caster it is vital that you understand the effects of the moon on the Earth and how they can influence your spells. Spells whether white or black work on spirits time with that in mind you should follow the spell as directed choosing the right day and correct time of day or night to ensure your spells potency.

Lastly, but most important, once the spell is cast forget about the spell, clear your mind with water or a crystal then wash your hands and or go outside to nature to release the energies and re-energize yourself. At this point the etheric weaving has been done. The rest is simply a matter of time.

MOON PHASES

The moon phases have long held a place of mystery and magic used to bring fourth desired outcomes. The benefit of incorporating the moon phases into your spell casting is to receive and release the most powerful energy into your spells. For maximum efficiency the intention of your spell should be in alignment with the appropriate moon phases, since each moon phase hold its own power and purpose indicative of the types of spells that are best suited to be cast during that moon cycle.

Certain moon phases are used purely for increase and other phases to decrease or remove unwanted energies. For instance if you're casting a spell to remove a bad habit or person from your life you would take advantage of the waning moons energy. The moon phases consists of five moon positions beginning with the new moon, waxing moon, full moon, waning moon and dark moon and blue moon.

The moon has the strongest effect on the outcomes of your spell casting. The full moon has the most power energy and effectiveness in spell casting due to its natural effect on the tides, emotions, actions. Our ancestors relied heavily upon the influence of the moon in their rituals and we continue today to integrate all elements of the spell to the phases of the moon. When spells are cast determines how effective the spell will be. The moon phases consist of a twenty-eight day lunar month, each phase of the moon transpires in seven day with the exception of the dark moon transpiring at three days. The following reflects the moon phases along with the appropriate spells to be cast during that particular moon phase.

New Moon The new moon is the birth of the lunar cycle reflecting an alignment with Earth and Sun. At this phase you only see the dark sky without an illuminating moon. The new moon is a most favorable time to cast spells relating to New beginnings, New career, New love, and to re-energize yourself.

Waxing Moon The waxing moon begins right after the new moon. At this phase the moon is becoming fuller, increasing as each day passes by. This is a time to cast spells to add something to your life that is lacking. The waxing moon is beneficial for health spells, inspiration, power, material things and games of chance and to find what you have lost.

Full Moon The full moon is at its most powerful magical state. For maximum potency ensure your spell is done the first day of the full moon. However you can still benefit from the full moon a few days before and after. The full moon favors a wide range of spells associated with guidance, projects and aspirations, love, marriage, clairvoyance and health. Best used for quick results and those of most importance. The full moon is used for black magic to evoke demons, call on the dead and hex enemies.

Waning Moon The waning moon is in a state of decrease occurring after the full moon. During this phase your spells should focus on spells to remove what is no longer wanted or needed in your life. Spells favored at this phase include getting rid of bad habits, negative energy, un-wanted people and ending relationships. Best used to make an enemy go away or for removing a bad spirit or eliminating slander along.

Blue Moon The blue moon refers to the occurrence of two moons in a one month time period. The blue moon is an auspicious time for good luck and reaching what is considered impossible. Favored spells include innovation, games of chance, and winning lottery jackpots.

Dark Moon - The Dark Moon occurs in the last three days of the lunar phase, right before the New Moon makes an appearance. The dark moon is a time for spells dealing with enhanced creativity, inventions, launching new brands, and new products. The dark moon reflects the notion that from the dark comes light and creation. The dark moon can be a time of reflection, retreat and healing thus it is best known as a time of transformation.

Within this dark moon we can reflect on who we are, who we have become and where we are headed and if any change needs to be made this is the perfect moon phase for it. The dark moon allows us to look deeper within to the core of our being. We tend to think of dark times in our lives as total disasters, However the opposite holds true, the dark times is the path that lead us to light to new exciting and favorable beginnings. The dark moon can be seen as a time of shedding off our old skins, habits, and thoughts leaving us with newfound wisdom and courage.th

THE PLANETS

The planets are crucial in our preparation and determination of the spell we are casting for each intention. The most powerful spells are cast with an awareness of planetary alignment in mind along with the moon phases and corresponding herbs that are linked to certain planets. Once this preparation is done the next consideration involves the days of the week and hour of the day to accurately intensify the effect of the spell. As noted below the planets influence certain areas of life and thus intentions should be clearly known and used accordingly to maximize the power of your spells.

PLANETS- DAYS OF THE WEEK

Moon (Monday) Travel, Spiritual Journey, Psychic Abilities, and Protection against attacks, Clairvoyance

Mars (Tuesday) Removing Negativity, Getting Rid of Enemies, Winning Judgments and access to the Spiritual World.

Mercury (Wednesday) Maintaining Wealth, Gaining Knowledge, Wisdom and Open Doors.

Jupiter (Thursday) Acquiring Riches, Favors, and Bringing Fourth Business Partner, Justice and Admiration.

Venus (Friday) Fertility, Love, Passion, Sex, Forcing Others To Come To You.

Saturn (Saturday) Business Success, Protect Home, Belongings

Sun (Sunday) Healing, Positive Energy, Invisibility and Attract Friends

THE ANGELS: CELESTIAL BEINGS

Angels were created of light since time began; they give fourth all we find to be benevolent and pure representing selflessness as they are sent to us as celestial spirits entrusted with super natural deeds to save those in dire need. Angles can travel at the speed of light between realms instilling in us thoughts of the eternal presence. Angels being elevated teach us to do the same through their actions.

As they say the fruit doesn't fall far from the tree, angels being elevated teach us to do the same to allow our actions to say who we are, letting them speak loudly and clearly. The angels and the world know us by our actions as they are gathered and stored transparently in the infinite, mirroring our true soul for time eternal. We hold the essence of the eternal presence within us making us higher beings with innate powers that have been bestowed upon us at our birth. Being created of the same essence as angels we have the ability to tap into and emulate their energy and contact the eternal presence at any time.

In white spell casting we can invoke the angels to guide and intercede for us. The angels are direct links to the eternal presence. The angels are always near us but they must be proactively summoned to allow us to gain insight, guidance and knowledge. Contacting the angels requires us to go inward they are fully aware of who we are and what we need. They have full knowledge of our entire life all the words and actions we have done and said. Angels are created with the highest level of love, thus they love you unconditionally.

By creating an altar in their honor you vividly open a visible door a direct link to the angels. Turning on a white candle is ideal being that light attracts light. Then simply call out to them and ask for guidance say, only the spirits called are welcomed. You can ask which angels are currently working with you and or any particular question you might have in mind, then keep your mind blank and wait for a response. Once you make contact you will feel warmth at this point write down any thoughts, words, color or feelings that come to you. Now, silence your mind and listen to any sounds as they identify themselves to you, every angel has distinct energy and tend to contact you in their own way.

Every person on Earth has various angels surrounding them at different points in their development and life experiences. There is a team of angels waiting to guide you so make the connection and get to know them. The angels can inspire and direct your spiritual journey bringing beneficial results from your white spell casting. Angels have the power to take the intentions of your spells to a higher power for instant manifestation due to their closeness to the eternal presence enabling you to make direct contact and your intentions known for maximum effectiveness. We are divine essence and when we connect with angels our spells are placed favorably to the highest level of ethereal vibration.

THE ANGELS

Seraphim (Crown Chakra) Highest Order of Angels, Nearest to the Eternal Presence, Purification, Remove Darkness, Cast out from Grace

Cherubim (Third Eye Chakra) All knowing, Holds Records/Score of the World, Guards

Thrones (All Seeing Eye) All Seeing Eye, Karma, Judgment

Dominions (Heart Chakra) Love, Intuition, Power over all

Michael (Solar Plexus Chakra) Defend, Struggle, War

Raphael (Solar Plexus Chakra) Healer Mind, Body, and Soul, Deception, Lies

Gabriel (Solar Plexus Chakra) Future, Good News, Joy

THE CHAKRAS

The chakras serve as a conductor offering us a gateway to a constant flow of optimum life energy that brings fourth the development of our self-consciousness creating a perfect fusion between our physical, mental and emotional self a benefit that can be synchronized into our spell casting rituals. In spell casting being connected and consciously aware of the clarity of the spell is a powerful key to unlock powerful spells. The chakra energy allows you to properly balance your spells by aligning the right energy.

Chakras are an alignment of the seven powerful vortexes that fuse into mind, body and spirit. To activate more power in your spells, stimulate the chakra energy that represents your intention. By infusing your spells with powerful chakra energy, you bring fourth manifestation power for prosperity, relationships, health, happiness and spiritual elevation. The chakras illuminate the mind harnessing your psychic powers to reach your genius state of power aligning the proper chakra energy to your spells can dispel infertility, sloth, illness, bad luck, remove obstacles, remove problems and remove your enemies of power. The chakras allow you to achieve balance and clarity of thought and direction.

The chakras transformative powers cleanse and uplift you to greater power in your spell casting, clearing any clouded lower level energy you might possess that can interfere with your spell. Chakra energy is vital in increasing your intuition and expanding your awareness to complimentary elements such as; herbs, precious stones, animal energies and angels that can empower spell casting.

By integrating all the elements with the balancing power of chakras you can create extremely potent spells, the resulting light potent energy that is birth from this powerful spell casting fusion. Spell casting through the use of the seven chakras allow you to manifest the conditions you desire from the intimacy of your private sacred place by personal alignment and the freeing of energies.

7 CHAKRAS

Root Chakra (Red) Foundations, New Beginnings

Sacral Chakra (Orange) Woman Issues, Infertility, Persistence

Solar Plexus (Yellow) Communicating Archangels, Letting go, Past, Personal Power

Heart Chakra (Green/Pink) Heart, Love, Compassion, Forgiveness, Balance

Throat Chakra (Light Blue) Communication, Confessions, Strength, Determination

Third Eye Chakra (Deep Purple) Eyes, Intuition, Truth, Understanding, Cherubim

Crown Chakra (Light Purple) Mind, Wisdom, Contact Seraphim, Plans, Inventions

THE STONES

Precious stones are birthed in the Earth and are induced with natural potent powerful energy, which has been used for ages in the magical arts for healing, safety, good luck, business, marriage and to remove bad habits. Nature itself holds the world's secrets each stone therefore is embedded with their own secret power, holding their particular force within. Certain stones have the power within them to calm the seas, silence the winds and diffuse the fires. By harnessing the innate energy of the stones we can personalize and increase the power of the spells.

Precious stones carry occult mystical properties that you can use as amulets by cleansing and charging the stone for your intention. By placing the stone in your hands you can immediately gain use of their power. Stones cleanse the body of negativity and then re-invigorate the body. Precious stones in spell casting increase the spells ability to bring love, wealth, health, connect to psychic abilities, dispel enemies, depression and invoke the underworld.

Agate- Insomnia, Induce Pleasant Dreams, and Visions

Alexandrite- Attracts Business Partners Due to its Rarity

Amazonite- Favors Long Relationships, Marriage

Amber- Inner Resemblance of an Eye, Favors protection spells against jealousy and envy

Amethyst- Favors spells to deter sickness, calming of the spirit

Aqua Marine- Due to its natural transparency favors divination, decisions, and education

Bloodstone- Favors healing blood related condition. Black magic to cause illness tragedy

Carnelian- Appears as hot lava favors circulatory concerns. Favors entertainers, singers, politicians, promotes self-confidence and passion

Crystals- Due to its ability to harness energy favors healing

Diamonds- Favors fame, fortune, and gaining power due to the strength of the stone

Emeralds- The green color of the stone and inclusions favors fertility

Fluorite- Magical stone favors spells to appease the mind, bring peace to the world, alertness, and stops sloth

Golden Beryl-Favors spells to gain power over enemies, manipulation

Hematite-Legal matters and judgments

Jade-Due to its hardening factor favors protection, completion spells

Lapiz-Lazuli-The deep intense color of this stone favors high power, status, royalty, heals vision, fever and depression and mental disturbances

Moonstone- Absorbs the power of the moon favors quick results, psychic ability, and luck

Obsidian-The beauty of the stone favors personal protection

Onyx-The Ying-yang brings light from darkness, release the old welcome the new, transformational stone

Opal- Due to its' softening aspect this stone favors changing a persons mind, forgiveness, second chances. In black magic spells to cause an enemy loss, interruption, ill health

Ruby-The power of this beautiful red stone favors protection of the womb, high morals, prevents accidents, a shield against poverty

Sapphire-This stone reflects the ocean within its power, favors truth, finding missing items, finding the culprit

Sodalite-Favors scholarly pursuits, graduation

Topaz-Due to its natural yellow color representative of the sun favors spells to increase health, healing pain and longevity

Turquoise-This stone favors life goals, accomplishment, spirituality and specifically to contact angels

THE TREES

Trees have a privileged place in spell casting they allow you to gather vital energy to fill your spirit with prior to casting a spell. Trees are used to release unwanted energy left over by a spell you casted or that has been cast upon you. Trees have a grounding nature since they are deeply rooted into Earth, allowing you to focus and clarity as to the intention of your spell. Trees solid connection to the earth allow you to cleanse yourself of energy that is no longer needed and at the same time allows you to re-energize yourself with new potent energy. This new copious energy will align you making all the difference in the spell you are preparing yourself to cast. The trees and their purpose in spell casting

1. Apple Trees- Happiness
2. Ash Trees-Strength
3. Aspen Trees-Persistence
4. Banyan Trees-Spirituality, enlightenment
5. Beech Trees- Knowledge
6. Birch Trees-Visions, New Paths
7. Bonsai Trees- Peace
8. Cedar Trees-Healing

9. Cherry Trees-Destruction, Death

10. Cypress Trees-Black Magic, invocations

11. Elder Trees-Divination

12. Oak Trees-Warrior, Triumphs

13. Palm Trees-Open Doors, Manifestation

THE HERBS

Herbs are born of the Earth offering Earthly properties that are beneficial to spell casting. The spells in this book use herbs in a myriad of ways in dressing candles they are sprinkled over essential oils or carried with you to obtain their power or fused with another powerful element. Herbs can be placed strategically around your home in open containers to energize and bring fourth money, harmony and remove negative influences.

Herbs are used in banishing and increasing spells. Herbs are potent allies in deterring evil forces, attracting love, power and bringing fourth health and wealth. In times passed herbs were solely used for their medicinal properties and spiritual elevation. Herbs have a high concentration of healing properties that bring the body mind and spirit back into alignment re-invigorating the soul.

Anise Seeds-To develop psychic powers, clairvoyance
Basil-For harmony and happiness in the home to repel depression
Bay Leaves-Dispel negative energy placed in the four corners of the home for protection of hexes and from the underworld. Bay leaves improve memory

Calendula-For legal matters, court triumphs

Cinnamon-To attract prosperity, leverage and good business partners

Devils Shoestring-Black magic spells to remove an enemy from your path, weaken the enemy and cause misfortune

Fennel Seeds-Placed in an the open brings wealth and abundance to the home

Garlic-Hung on your front door to repel all negative influences from their home

Guinea Pepper- Favors black magic spells, cause fights, wars, break up all types of relationships and marriages

High John-Favors a good life, triumph over enemies, completion, wishes and career

Kava Kava-Favors black magic spells for communication with the underworld, to cause misunderstanding, disruption and destruction

Lavender-To calm the mind, body, and spirit Forgiveness second chances

Licorice Sticks-Protection from the unknown, accidents and misfortune

Marjoram-Protection from curses and the underworld carry with you

Poppy Seeds-For divination, to control others, to bind someone to you

Rosemary-To encourage good vibrations when you have visitors, simply burn a small amount of rosemary in the room where the visitors will be seated.

Sage-Removes negativity due to its purifying effect, use in the home when the energy seems heavy. Sage in a smudge stick to cleanse a person from their past, depression and sloth

Sesame Seeds- For Prosperity and business ventures. Place at the right side of the door of your home or business.

Slippery Elm-To Increase favorable communication and stop slander

Soloman's Seal-Used for exorcism, to dispel dark forces, removing hexes

Yerba Santa- For spiritual power against the underworld

THE OILS

In this book candles will be dressed with oils to serve as a powerful foundation in spell casting. Oils have been used for anointing since ancient times. Oils will be fused together to increase the potency of the spells. Our sense of smell is very powerful tool and serves to open our minds to the spirit world allowing us to see passed the Earth into the divine, where spells are manifested.

Oils must be of natural synthetic oils should be avoided when possible. It is good practice to conjure your own oils to embed your individual energy into the oils. Your rituals and spells will be best served with natural self-prepared oils. Oils are the direct link to the spiritual world to the unseen world and therefore instrumental in opening the doors to the higher realm allowing our spell to be manifested quickly and effectively.

Cubeb Berries- Make Yourself Desirable, youth spells

Frankincense Oil- Best used as blessing oil

Ginseng Oil- To Gain power and control enemies

High John Oil- For success in business, love, career, to conquer

Holy Oil- Best used for exorcisms against the underworld

Lemon Verbena- Cause conflict, separations

Myrrh Oil-Blessing oil fused with frankincense for maximum potency

Patchouli Oil- For a lover to return

Rose Oil- Attract love

Sarsaparilla-Prolong Life

Thyme Oil- Gain respect and honor

Vervain Oil- Arouse passion

THE CANDLES

Candles represent the fire element in spell casting bringing fiery ardent passion to spells. Depending on the intention of the spell candles can be dressed with oils and herbs to gather more powerful results. Always dress candles from the top down then in an upward direction. Candles can be used to raise your vibration and energy level thru visualization to reach a higher plateau in spell casting to create the right ambiance and elemental factor for potency in your spells. Candles for the purposes of this book should be virgin new candles, as any residue of energy from previous spells will disrupt the effectiveness of the spell.

Black- Dispel Negative Energy, Invocation, Shape Shifting

Blue- Water, Open Doors, Communication, Clarity, and Wisdom

Brown- Grounding, Special Favors

Copper- Longevity in Business, Promotion

Dark Red- Wars

Gold- Wealth, Winning, and Abundance

Green- Earth, Growth, Fertility, and Financial Success

Gray- Neutralize, Balance, Remove Past

Orange- Buy New Property, Career and Legal Matters

Pink- Romance, Good Will, Friendship

Purple- Expansion, Influence, Psychic and Spiritual Power

Red- Fire, Attraction, Passion

Silver- Air, Clairvoyance, Telepathy, Dreams

White- Spirituality, Peace, Harmony, and Unity

Yellow- Genius, Graduation, Confidence

THE TAROT CARDS

MAJOR ARCANA

1. **Chariot-**Time of War, struggle, triumph over Enemies,
2. **Death-**All Endings, Transformation
3. **Devil-**All Worldly Pleasure, Rebellion, Ambition, Addiction
4. **Emperor-**Enthusiasm, Misused Power
5. **Empress-**Creator, Nourishing, Inventor, Abundance
6. **Fool-**All is Laid out for success, Pay Attention, Warning
7. **Hanged Man-**Loss Honor, Stuck, In Time Suspension
8. **Hermit-**Introverted, No Action then comes Enlightenment
9. **Hierophants-**Awakening, Spirituality, Esoteric Realm, Cruel
10. **High Priestess-**Invention, Holder of Vital Secrets, Grand Idea
11. **Judgment-**Sins Forgiven, Rebirth, Remove from Honor
12. **Justice-**Excesses, Consequences, Court Cases, Legal Documents
13. **Lovers-**Gemini, Two Choices, Something Coming
14. **Magician-**Sales Person, Politician, Trickster, Conman, Fraud
15. **Moon-**Visions, Genius, Psychic Powers, Warning Hidden Enemies, addictions

MINOR ARCANA

1. **Star**-The Future, Achievements, Wrong Path, Obstacles
2. **Strength**-Powerful, Inner Strength, Vengeful, Lust
3. **Sun**-Triumph, Truth, Youthfulness, What's Wrong is Righted,
4. **Temperance**-Transformation, Moving Forward
5. **Tower**-War, False Guidance, Destruction, Falls Through
6. **Wheel of Fortune**-Abundance, Karma, Lottery Win, Reversal of Fortune
7. **World**-Complete, Graduation, Celebrate, World Travel, Long Journey
8. **Ace of Wands**-New Interest
9. **Ace of Cups**-New Love, Emotions
10. **Ace of Swords**-Alertness, Mental Agility
11. **Ace of Pentacles**-New Paths Opening in All Directions
12. **Two of Wands**-Choices, Passion
13. **Two of Cups**-Recognition, Honor Awareness
14. **Two of Swords**-Conflicting Sides and Opinions
15. **Two of Pentacles**-Juggling, switching Back and Fourth
16. **Three of Wands**-Fruition, Waiting for Harvest
17. **Three of Cups**-Celebrations, Family, Reunions

18. **Three of Swords-**Broken Heart, Love Triangles, Harsh Words

19. **Three of Pentacles-**Developing, Apprentice, Positive Results, Health

20. **Four of Wands-**Solid Foundation, Marriage

21. **Four of Cups-**Lack of satisfaction, Taking Things for Granted

22. **Four of Swords-**Healing, Recuperating, Rest, Retrospect

23. **Four of Pentacles-**Penny Pincher, Comfort, Balance Life

24. **Five of Wands-**Power Struggle, Conflict, Competition

25. **Five of Cups-**Past, Regrets

26. **Five of Swords-**Winning Fights, Knowing when to avoid fights

27. **Five of Pentacles-**Bad Luck, Doors Closed, Final, Loss

28. **Six of Wands-**Triumphant, Boldness, High Regard, beat the Odds

29. **Six of Cups-**Joy, Nostalgia, Old Friend

30. **Six of Swords-**Travel, Change of Scenery

31. **Six of Pentacles-**Generosity, Boon, Scholarship, Grant

32. **Seven of Wands-**Odds piled against you, Under Attack, Defend Yourself

33. **Seven of Cups-**Pulled in Many Directions, Mixed emotions

34. **Seven of Swords-**Surprise Attack, Stolen Inventions

35. **Seven of Pentacles-**Harvest, Waiting Period, Patience

36. **Eight of Wands-**Quick Manifestation, Timing, Wise use of Energy

37. **Eight of Cups-**Current Path brought you down, Excesses

38. **Eight of Swords-**Fear overwhelming, Immobile, Communicate

39. **Eight of Pentacles-Newness,** New beginnings, New Exercise Routine

40. **Nine of Wands-**Invest the energy in yourself, Summit, Success

41. **Nine of Cups-**Joyful Interactions, What you put in you get out

42. **Nine of Swords-**Anxiety, Insomnia, Nightmares, Problems

43. **Nine of Pentacles-**Invest in You, No luxury yet comfortable

44. **Tens of Wands-**Leader, Boss, Burden by responsibility

45. **Tens of Cups-**Emotional Support, Happiness, Reunions

46. **Tens of Swords-**End of Arguments, Disagreements

47. **Tens of Pentacles-**Abundance, Inheritance

THE ELEMENTS

The elements air, water, earth, fire are essential to our planet Earth. The world's natural elements consist air, fire, water and earth. These elements are the foundation of our planet and are essential in spell casting. The elements energetic properties are chosen by their position and properties to maximize the spell according to the intention of the spell.

ELEMENTS	PROPERTIES	COLOR	POSITIONS
Air	Communication	Yellow	East
Water	Invention, Emotions	Blue	West
Earth	Abundance, Prosperity Protect home, Children	Green	North
Fire	Passion, Longevity	Red	South

Fire

Fire is directed energy that can be used for white or black magic depending on the nature of the spell. Spells requiring masculine energy will benefit from this element. In spells where the sun is ruling as the governing planet the fire element should be primary. Fire in white magic is best to ignite passion in a relationship or bring fast money and or helpful people to your life. Fire in black magic can be used to destroy an enemy home, harvest and business. Fire is strong powerful and dominating yang energy. Candles can be placed on your altar to represent the fire element.

Earth

The Earth energy is a grounding stabilizing element favors spells requiring strong foundations. Spells to marry, have children, buy a new home, and or new career would be under this element. The earth is filled with the power of fertility making it yin energy bringing fourth a nurturing nature that favors creation allowing us to manifest our desires. The earth element is best for spells to promote gain and longevity. Herbs and stones can be placed in your altar to represent Earth.

Water

The water element has a calming effect aimed toward bringing harmony to the home, forgiveness. The water element relates to emotions and favors spells to releasing ill feelings, letting go, and moving forward. Water can be used for healing spells and to protect against insomnia. Spells for long voyages, world travel and ocean liner cruises make best use of the water element. To represent water on your altar you can place aquamarine stone or chalice filled with rainwater.

Air

The element of air represents transitions, temporary situations, fluidity, agility and quick manifestations. In spell casting air favors travel mainly short trips by plane or car, independence, invisibility, swiftness, and alertness. The air element due to its nature is favored for spells to dispel rage, bad feelings and all negative energy. On your altar you can place a wand to represent air.

THE ANIMAL PRESENCE

The animal's presence allows you to visualize the energy you must draw upon to conjure a potent spell. Due to their closeness to nature animals hold many of the Earths secrets and certain cycles that are beneficial in spell casting. Invoking an animal presence when you cast the spell allows you to hone in on their energy and power. The animal presence gives us access to hidden knowledge that is innate to them. The animal presence in white spells favors spells for elevation, courage, action, invisibility and monogamy. In black magic used to destroy enemies, invoke demons, access to the underworld. Once you allow yourself to connect with nature you will have access to guidance, warnings, triumph and insight from a time long passed. All winged animals dictate manifestation and new heights in general.

ANT - Ability to prosper ten fold

BALD EAGLE - Gained power, wisdom of the ages

BAT - Creation

BEE - Build, new projects, career

CRANE - Pact with the devil

CROW - Full potential, guardian, protector, secret knowledge

DRAGONFLY - Mental disturbances

DUCKS - Cash flow, boon, comfort

EAGLES - Honor, reward, new life

GOOSE - Travel, adventure

GRASSHOPPER - Auspicious good luck, Boon

HAWKS - Visionary, psychic abilities

HUMMINGBIRDS - Accomplish more than others, extraordinary, true love

INSECTS - Irritation, problems, enemies around you

OWL - Black and white magic, woman issues, prophecy, wisdom, hidden data

REDTAIL HAWK - Speak to the departed and tear down enemies

ROOSTER - Arouse passion, center of attention, sexuality

SEA GULLS - Communicate with other realms, explorer

SHORT-EARED OWL - Ambush, fearless and resourceful

SPIDERS - Opportunities abound, adventure, exploration

SWANS- Marriage, Monogamy

WOLF - Long voyage, rewards, self-confident, independent

CREATING YOUR ALTAR

The altar will be a place where you commune with the spiritual world through spell casting. An altar should be created when you are in a relaxed state of clarity as the elements you choose can influence your intentions. The altar should be individualized to your style and current intention of the spell. The altar is a place of power where you can conjure spells and cast them. There are exceptions when certain spells must be cast outdoors in nature near a tree, in a historic building, temple, mission, crossroads or cemetery widely dependent on the intention and nature of the spell.

The alter must be dedicated to a deity source as the offerings and elements for the spell must be in alignment to reach maximum power. The altar itself can be made of any material you feel a connection to such as wood or iron. The altar should be of good size to allow room for comfort to cast your spells and allow personalization. The altar must reflect your style and be made to honor your source, Buddah, Angels or Green Man or the elements air, fire, water, Earth. Paying homage to the elements is crucial to cementing your intentions adding powerful energy to your spell casting. The more familiar you are with your source or entity the more you can add to increase its power, then place your offerings and spell casting tools upon it. Be open to your intention when decorating your altar a new twist might be the key to instant manifestation.

Begin by blessing your altar and energizing it with your energy. You can lite a white sage smudge stick to smudge your altar. The altar must be energized periodically for potent spell casting specially when casting a new spell to create harmony and the right energy for the new spell. You can re-energize the altar by sprinkling water over it or by lighting a smudge stick on your altar when you feel its energy low. Your altar must be well cared for to render potency. Place your altar in a secluded area of your home to focus on your spell casting.

WHITE MAGIC SPELLS

INTENTION: ATTRACT LOVE

1. Moon Phase: New Moon
2. Day of the week: Friday
3. Time of day: Evening
4. Governing Planet: Venus
5. Angels: Dominions
6. Chakras: Heart
7. Precious Stones: Rose Quartz
8. Tarot Card: Empress
9. Candles: Pink
10. Oils: Cardomom Oil, Rosemary Oil
11. Herbs: Orris Root, Senna Leaf, and Violet Leaf
12. Trees: Apple Tree
13. Animal presence: Humming Bird

THE SPELL

On the night of a new moon light a pink candle for romance. Fill your bath water with cardamom oil, rosemary oil, and rose oil as you add the oils use your right hand to stir the oils with your finger in clockwise direction. Add Orris root, Senna leaf and Violet leaf to the water soak for fifteen minutes imagining what your new lover will look like then lightly scrub your body with sugar, rinse. Wear something pink.

INTENTION: CHOOSE THE RIGHT LOVER

1. Moon Phase: New Moon
2. Day of the week: Friday
3. Time of day: Evening
4. Governing Planet: Venus
5. Angels: Dominion
6. Chakras: Root
7. Precious Stones: Rose quartz, Sapphire
8. Tarot Card: Two of Wands
9. Candles: Pink, Red
10. Oils: Lotus Oil
11. Herbs: Angelica, Dittany of Crete
12. Trees: Apple Tree
13. Animal presence: Fox

THE SPELL

On the night of a new moon write the names of those lovers interested in you on a few shelled walnuts. Anoint your hands with lotus oil then go outdoors to light a fire with stick matches. When the fire reaches its optimum throw a handful of salt to the fire, as it turns blue the energy is purified offering clarity. Throw the walnuts into the fire and notice the first one to pop or be wildly consumed in the fire revealing the right lover.

INTENTION: TO MAINTAIN LOVE

1. Moon Phase: Full Moon
2. Day of the week: Friday
3. Time of day: Evening
4. Governing Planet: Venus
5. Angels: Dominion
6. Chakras: Root
7. Precious Stones: Rose Quartz
8. Tarot Card: Four of Wands
9. Candles: Red
10. Oils: Rose Oil
11. Herbs: Rosemary, Raspberry Leaves, and Skullcap
12. Trees: Aspen
13. Animal presence: Pigeon

THE SPELL

On the night of a full moon light a red candle dressed with rose oil. Place the four of Wands next to the candle with rose quartz in front of the candle. Find willowy rosemary branches that can be bent to the shape of your lover's first initial then bind it with red yarn and keep in your undergarment drawer.

INTENTION: AROUSE PASSION IN YOUR LOVER

1. Moon Phase: Full Moon
2. Day of the week: Friday
3. Time of day: Evening
4. Governing Planet: Venus
5. Angels: Dominions
6. Chakras: Root
7. Precious Stones: Copper, Inca Rose stone
8. Tarot Card: Two of Wands
9. Candles: Red
10. Oils: Lavender Oil, Red Pepper Oil
11. Herbs: Rose petals, Cubeb Berries and Cardamom
12. Trees: Apple Tree
13. Animal presence: Rooster

THE SPELL

On the darkest night of a full moon light a large red candle dressed in red pepper oil. Place the two of wands on the left side of the candle and a rose stone on the right. You will need your lover's undergarment to place a copper penny in the center along with red pepper, Cubeb berries and Rose petals. As you fold the undergarment make sure you make the folds toward you, then place the undergarment with your personal items where it will not be found. Passion will storm in, be ready.

INTENTION: TO BECOME ENGAGED

1. Moon Phase: Full Moon
2. Day of the week: Friday
3. Time of day: Evening
4. Governing Planet: Venus
5. Angels: Dominion
6. Chakras: Heart
7. Precious Stones: Diamond, lodestone
8. Tarot Card: Four of Wands
9. Candles: Pink, Red
10. Oils: Holy oil, Lavender oil and Rose oil
11. Herbs: Rosemary, Spikenard, and Magnolia leaves
12. Trees: Apple Tree
13. Animal presence: Red Tail Hawk

THE SPELL

On the night of a full moon light a red and pink candle both dressed with three drops of holy oil, three drops of lavender oil and three drops of rose oil. Between the candles place the four of wands with magnolia leaves on top. On parchment paper write your name with your lovers surname and place under your pillow for twenty-one days. Boil a cup of water then add rose petals when cooled place into new container to be used daily over your heart. You will need a photograph of your lover and your self then place them together with your eyes looking at each other and bind it with red yarn.

INTENTION: TO MARRY

1. Moon Phase: Full Moon
2. Day of the week: Friday
3. Time of day: Evening
4. Governing Planet: Venus
5. Angels: Dominion
6. Chakras: Heart
7. Precious Stones:
8. Tarot Card:
9. Candles: Pink
10. Oils: Lavender Oil, Rose Oil
11. Herbs: Cubeb Berries
12. Trees: Pine tree
13. Animal presence: Swans

THE SPELL

On a night of a full moon in the month of December only, Light a pink candle dress with Lavender oil and Rose oil. Buy a small white pine tree, anoint the tree trunk with rose oil, lavender oil and cubeb berries and decorate the pine tree with white ribbons. On parchment paper write your name with the surname of the person you want to marry in dove's blood, place at the base of the tree. Marriage will come very soon

INTENTION: BECOME PREGNANT

1. Moon Phase: New Moon
2. Day of the week: Monday
3. Time of day: Evening
4. Governing Planet: Moon
5. Angels: Gabriel
6. Chakras: Sacral
7. Precious Stone: Unakite, Azurite, and Coral
8. Tarot Card: The Star
9. Candles: White
10. Oils: Juniper Berry Oil, Sandalwood Oil
11. Herbs: Cubeb Berries,
12. Trees: Aspen
13. Animal presence: Rabbit

THE SPELL

On the evening of a new moon light a white candle dressed with four drops of juniper berry oil and five drops of sandalwood oil. Place the star card on the front of the candle. On an egg make a small whole and add cubeb berries to it then go to your garden and bury it. To invoke rabbit energy, bring children into your home the next day have them jump on your bed to energize your bed with fertility energy.

INTENTION: GIVE BIRTH TO A GIRL

1. Moon Phase: New Moon

2. Day of the week: Monday

3. Time of day: Morning

4. Governing Planet: Moon

5. Angels: Gabriel

6. Chakras: Sacral

7. Precious Stone: Unakite, Coral

8. Tarot Card: Empress

9. Candles: White, Pink

10. Oils: Gardenia Oil, Rosemary Oil

11. Herbs: Partridge Berry, Angelica

12. Trees: Apple Tree

13. Animal presence: Calico Cat

THE SPELL

To encourage the birth of a girl light a white and pink candle dressed in rose petal oil sprinkled with angelica. Place the empress card on the right side of the candle. On parchment paper in doves ink write I have a daughter then place under the empress card. Make a small doll and add your picture to the face area and add hair from your brush to the hair area of the doll to engender a daughter. Light the candles daily for nine days and will a girl to you.

INTENTION: GIVE BIRTH TO A BOY

1. Moon Phase: Full Moon
2. Day of the week: Sunday
3. Time of day: Midday
4. Governing Planet: The Sun
5. Angels: Gabriel
6. Chakras: Sacral
7. Precious Stones: Unakite, Coral and Quartz
8. Tarot Card: Magician
9. Candles: White, Blue, and Yellow
10. Oils: Frankincense Oil,
11. Herbs: Partridge Berry, Papoose Root, and Burdock Root
12. Trees: Apple Tree
13. Animal presence: Peacock

THE SPELL

To encourage the birth of a boy light a white, blue and yellow candle dressed in frankincense oil sprinkled with partridgeberry. Place the blue candle on the left the yellow candle on the right and the white candle on top at the tip of the triangle. Place the magician card and a peacock feather in the center of the candles. On parchment paper in doves ink write I have a son and place underneath the magician card. Relight the candles for three days in a row at the same hour. Nightly before going to sleep think of the peacock and see yourself holding a baby boy in your arms.

INTENTION: BUY THE RIGHT HOUSE

1. Moon Phase: New Moon
2. Day of the week: Saturday
3. Time of day: Morning
4. Governing Planet: The sun
5. Angels: Dominion
6. Chakras: Root
7. Precious Stones: Sapphire
8. Tarot Card: Three of Cups
9. Candles: Blue, Gold
10. Oils: Basil Oil, Wisteria Oil
11. Herbs: Alfalfa, Blessed Thistle and Blood Root
12. Trees: Apple Tree
13. Animal presence: Turtle

THE SPELL

On a new moon light a blue candle with wisteria oil and gold candle with basil oil sprinkle both with blessed thistle. Place the three of cups between the candles. Invoke the turtle energy to assist you in finding the right house. In a small satchel add alfalfa and bloodroot along with an image of a turtle and keep it with you as you look for a house. You will attract the right house to you.

INTENTION: HARMONY IN THE HOME

1. Moon Phase: Waxing Moon
2. Day of the week: Friday
3. Time of day: Evening
4. Governing Planet: Venus
5. Angels: Dominions
6. Chakras: Heart
7. Precious Stones: Agate, Amazonite
8. Tarot Card: Hierophant
9. Candles: Blue
10. Oils: Basil oil, Pennyroyal Oil
11. Herbs: Marjoram, Passionflower, and Lavender, and Pearl Moss
12. Trees: Bonsai
13. Animal presence: Humming Bird

THE SPELL

On the evening of a waxing moon, light a blue candle dressed with lavender and pennyroyal oil. Place the hierophant card on the left side of the candle and on the right side an image of a hummingbird sprinkled with passionflower. Now on the East side of the home keep a bonsai plant sprinkled with pearl moss, peace and harmony will be felt by all who live in and enter your home.

INTENTION: PROSPERITY IN THE HOME

1. Moon Phase: Full Moon
2. Day of the week: Thursday
3. Time of day: Evening
4. Governing Planet: Jupiter
5. Angels: Gabriel
6. Chakras: Crown
7. Precious Stones: Onyx, Jade
8. Tarot Card: Wheel of Fortune
9. Candles: Green
10. Oils: Basil Oil, Bayberry Oil
11. Herbs: Rice, Lentils, and Fenugreek
12. Trees: Palm Tree
13. Animal presence: Cricket

THE SPELL

On the night of a full moon light a green candle dressed in Basil and Bayberry oil place the wheel of fortune card on the right side of the candle. Invoke the angel Gabriel then fill an open container with fenugreek seeds letting it fill the air in your home with abundance and prosperity. The cricket energy has been energized.

INTENTION: ATTRACT MONEY

1. Moon Phase: Waxing moon
2. Day of the week: Thursday
3. Time of day: Evening
4. Governing Planet: Jupiter
5. Angels: Gabriel
6. Chakras: Throat
7. Precious Stones: Onyx, Jade, and Emerald
8. Tarot Card: Queen of Pentacles
9. Candles: Green, Yellow
10. Oils: Allspice Oil, Patchouli Oil
11. Herbs: Wintergreen, Bayberry Root, and Snake Lily
12. Trees: Palm Tree
13. Animal presence: Grasshopper

THE SPELL

On a waxing moon, light a green candle dress it with allspice and patchouli carve the amount of money you desire on the candle. Place the queen of pentacles in front of the candle on top of palm tree leaves with a jade stone on it. As you watch the flame envision the angel Gabriel assisting you in receiving money into your home. Place a mat in private, inside of your front door with wintergreen, bayberry root and a twenty-dollar bill under your mat, as you step on it every day the money rolls in.

INTENTION: PROTECT YOUR HOME

1. Moon Phase: Full Moon
2. Day of the week: Saturday
3. Time of day: Evening
4. Governing Planet: The Sun
5. Angels: Michael
6. Chakras: Third Eye
7. Precious Stones: Jasper
8. Tarot Card: Four of Pentacles
9. Candles: White, Yellow
10. Oils: Basil Oil, Coconut Oil
11. Herbs: Masters root, Syrian root, and Garlic cloves
12. Trees: Apple Tree
13. Animal presence: Crow, Wolf

THE SPELL

On the night of a full moon light a yellow candle dressed in basil oil, and a white candle dressed in coconut oil then sprinkle masters root, Syrian root on them. Place the four of pentacles between the candles. Envision the angel Michael's presence protecting your home plant garlic around the perimeter of your home to be protected.

INTENTION: DETER UNWANTED VISITORS

1. Moon Phase: Waning Moon
2. Day of the week: Tuesday
3. Time of day: Evening
4. Governing Planet: Mars
5. Angels: Michael
6. Chakras: Throat
7. Precious Stones: Agate
8. Tarot Card: Ten of swords
9. Candles: Black
10. Oils: Black pepper oil
11. Herbs: Boldo leaf, Broom Straw, Salt and Guinea pepper
12. Trees: Cypress
13. Animal presence: Skunk

THE SPELL

On the night of a waning moon light a black candle dress it with black pepper oil, as you look into the flames envision the presence of the skunk and it's repelling smell.

Place a broom with the bristles up on the left side of your door, sprinkle with guinea pepper, and boldo leaf on the broom bristles. Spell is cast.

INTENTION: DETER A PET FROM WANDERING

1. Moon Phase: Waxing Moon
2. Day of the week: Sunday
3. Time of day: Morning
4. Governing Planet: The Sun
5. Angels: Dominion
6. Chakras: Heart
7. Precious Stones: Turquoise
8. Tarot Card: Hierophant
9. Candles: Pink
10. Oils: Iris Oil
11. Herbs: Star Anise
12. Trees: Birch
13. Animal presence: Fox

THE SPELL

On the morning of a waxing moon, light a pink candle dressed in iris oil and star anise. Place a turquoise stone on the right side of the candle with a blue ribbon. Hold your pet and give it love now place butter on the bottom of your pets feet to deter wandering. Once the candle burns out take the blue ribbon and place it where your pet sleeps, your pet will stay with you.

INTENTION: FIND YOUR MISSING CAT

1. Moon Phase: Full Moon
2. Day of the week: Saturday
3. Time of day: Evening
4. Governing Planet: Saturn
5. Angels: Cherubim
6. Chakras: Crown
7. Precious Stones: Opal
8. Tarot Card:
9. Candles: Blue
10. Oils: Frankincense
11. Herbs: Catnip
12. Trees: Birch Tree
13. Animal presence: Grasshopper, Cat

THE SPELL

On the night of a full moon or sooner if you cannot wait that log, light a blue candle dressed in frankincense and sprinkled with catnip. In your mind's eye place a blue light around your cat. Place your hands in prayer position then move your hands apart slowly in opposite directions as you do make contact with your pet, see into their eyes, tell your pet to come back to you, your pet will come back to you swiftly.

INTENTION: FIND A MISSING ITEM

1. Moon Phase: Full Moon
2. Day of the week: Thursday
3. Time of day: Morning
4. Governing Planet: Jupiter
5. Angels: Cherubim
6. Chakras: Third Eye
7. Precious Stones: Sapphire
8. Tarot Card: Chariot
9. Candles: Brown
10. Oils: High John Oil
11. Herbs: Star Anise, Bay leaf, and Rose
12. Trees: Aspen
13. Animal presence: Grasshopper

THE SPELL

On the morning of a full moon light a brown candle and dress it with high john oil and sprinkle star anise gather an image of a grasshopper sprinkle rose petals over it and place it on the windowsill pointing in the direction of where your item last was. Sit in silence by the candle and watch the flame ponder on the happiness the item brought you and use your will power to bring it to you. As the flame gets bigger draw it to you. Invoke cherubim, as record holder will assist you in showing you where your item is. Place the chariot card in front of the candle with a rose petal on it for its quick return to you.

INTENTION: FIND WHO HAS YOUR MISSING ITEM

1. Moon Phase: Full Moon
2. Day of the week: Thursday
3. Time of day: Morning
4. Governing Planet: Jupiter
5. Angels: Cherubim
6. Chakras: Third Eye
7. Precious Stones: Sapphire
8. Tarot Card: Chariot
9. Candles: Brown
10. Oils: High John Oil
11. Herbs: Star Anise, Bay leaf and Rose
12. Trees: Aspen
13. Animal presence: Grasshopper

THE SPELL

On the morning of a full moon light a brown candle dress with high john oil and sprinkle star anise. On an image of a grasshopper add rose petals placing it on the windowsill in the direction where your item last was. On parchment paper in doves blood write the name of who you believe took your item place it under the chariot card add two rose petals on top of the card and invoke cherubim, as record holder will assist you in showing you who has your item. Place the chariot card in front of the candle with a rose petal on it for its quick return to you, if no result in nine-day change to another name.

INTENTION: STOP GOSSIP OR SLANDER

1. Moon Phase: Waning Moon
2. Day of the week: Wednesday
3. Time of day: Evening
4. Governing Planet: Mercury
5. Angels: Seraphim
6. Chakras: Throat
7. Precious Stones: Golden Berryl
8. Tarot Card: Seven of Swords
9. Candles: Black
10. Oils: Cinnamon Oil, Myrrh Oil
11. Herbs: Lemon Verbena, Aloes Powder, Slippery Elm and Chia
12. Trees: Cypress
13. Animal presence: Fox

THE SPELL

On the night of a waning moon on a black candle write the name of the person speaking against you, dress with cinnamon oil and sprinkle with aloes powder, lemon verbena. Wash your hands and anoint them with myrrh oil. In a flannel red bag carry slippery elm and chia with you to prevent others from speaking against you.

INTENTION: WIN IN COURT

1. Moon Phase: Full Moon
2. Day of the week: Saturday
3. Time of day: Evening
4. Governing Planet: Saturn
5. Angels: Seraphim
6. Chakras: Crown
7. Precious Stones: Ruby, Hematite
8. Tarot Card: Justice
9. Candles: Brown
10. Oils: High John
11. Herbs: Chewing John, Licorice Root, Deer Tongue, and Calendula
12. Trees: Oak tree
13. Animal presence: Crow, Spiders

THE SPELL

On the night of the full moon light a brown candle dressed with high john oil and sprinkled with licorice root and deer tongue. On parchment paper write the name of the judge with your name alongside in doves blood ink sprinkle with rose petals. Then write your enemies names spelled backwards on parchment with dragons blood ink. Go to a fast moving river and throw their names in and watch as they go away from you. Then wash your hands in water and add high john oil to your palms, head, and feet. On an oak tree leaf add a drop of high John and keep it with you until the next full moon.

INTENTION: AVOID GOING TO COURT

1. Moon Phase: Full Moon
2. Day of the week: Saturday
3. Time of day: Evening
4. Governing Planet: Saturn
5. Angels: Seraphim
6. Chakras: Crown
7. Precious Stones: Ruby, Hematite
8. Tarot Card: Justice
9. Candles: Brown, Orange
10. Oils: High John
11. Herbs: Chewing John, Licorice Root, and Calendula, Celadine
12. Trees: Oak tree
13. Animal presence: Crow, spiders

THE SPELL

On the night of the full moon light an orange candle dressed with high john oil and sprinkled with Calendula and deer tongue. On parchment paper write the name of the adversary backwards in dragons blood. Go to a fast moving river and throw the name in the river. Then wash your hands in water and add nine drops of high john oil to your palms, head, and feet.

INTENTION: PROTECTION AGAINST LAW ENFORCEMENT

1. Moon Phase: Full Moon

2. Day of the week: Tuesday

3. Time of day: Evening

4. Governing Planet: Mars

5. Angels: Seraphim

6. Chakras: Crown

7. Precious Stones: Obsidian

8. Tarot Card: Two of Wands

9. Candles: Black

10. Oils: Mint Oil, Marjoram Oil

11. Herbs: Tansy, Asafoetida, Celadine and Fennel seeds

12. Trees: Oak Tree

13. Animal presence: Fox

THE SPELL

On the night of a full moon light a black anointed with marjoram oil and orange candle anointed with mint oil. Place asafetida in your car and also in a red flannel bag carry with you a mixture of celadine, tansy and fennel seeds.

INTENTION: PROTECT YOUR VALUABLES

1. Moon Phase: Full Moon
2. Day of the week: Sunday
3. Time of day: Evening
4. Governing Planet: The Sun
5. Angels: Michael
6. Chakras: Third Eye
7. Precious Stones: Jasper
8. Tarot Card: Four of pentacles
9. Candles: Yellow
10. Oils: Basil Oil, Eucalyptus Oil
11. Herbs: Plantain Leaf, Sage, and Marjoram
12. Trees: Oak Tree
13. Animal presence: Crow, Wolf

THE SPELL

On the night of a full moon light a yellow candle dressed in basil oil, eucalyptus oil then sprinkle sage, plantain leaf and marjoram over it. Place the four of pentacles on the right side of the candle. Envision the angel Michael's protecting your valuables then sprinkle salt around the perimeter of your home to be protected.

INTENTION: WARD OFF ENEMIES

1. Moon Phase: Full Moon
2. Day of the week: Tuesday
3. Time of day: Evening
4. Governing Planet: Mars
5. Angels: Cherubim
6. Chakras: Third Eye
7. Precious Stones: Ruby
8. Tarot Card: Chariot
9. Candles: Black
10. Oils: Vertivert Oil
11. Herbs: Rue, Rosemary, Broom straws, and Mustard seeds
12. Trees: Oak tree
13. Animal presence: Wolf

THE SPELL

On a full moon light a black candle anointed with vertivert oil. Plant garlics in the perimeter of your home then on the four corners of your property a handful of broom straws must be placed in each direction. Your enemies will not come near you.

INTENTION: WARD OFF DANGER

1. Moon Phase: Full Moon
2. Day of the week: Tuesday
3. Time of day: Evening
4. Governing Planet: Mars
5. Angels: Cherubim
6. Chakras: Third Eye
7. Precious Stones: Ruby
8. Tarot Card: Fool
9. Candles: Black
10. Oils: Ginger Oil
11. Herbs: Wormwood, fever few
12. Trees: Ash
13. Animal presence: Fox

THE SPELL

On the night of a full moon light a black candle anointed with ginger oil place the fool card on the right side of the candle sprinkle ash tree leaves over it. In a white flannel bag carry wormwood and fever few with you to ward off danger.

INTENTION: TRIUMPH OVER ENEMIES

1. Moon Phase: Full Moon
2. Day of the week: Tuesday
3. Time of day: Evening
4. Governing Planet: Mars
5. Angels: Seraphim
6. Chakras: Crown
7. Precious Stones: Emerald
8. Tarot Card: Chariot
9. Candles: Purple
10. Oils: Bergamont Oil, Calamus Oil
11. Herbs: Calamus Root, Sulphur, and Master of the Woods
12. Trees: Oak Tree
13. Animal presence: Fox

THE SPELL

On the night of a full moon light a black candle anoint with eight drops of calamus oil one drop of bergamot dress with master of the woods and calamus root. Place the chariot card on the right side of the candle. Make a wax figurine gather a strand of hair of the enemy or clothing adding it to the wax with a spoonful of sulphur. When hardened stand in front of the bathroom with your right hand crush the figurine completely and flush it down the toilet. Your triumph will come swiftly.

INTENTION: TO BE FORGIVEN

1. Moon Phase: New Moon
2. Day of the week: Tuesday
3. Time of day: Evening
4. Governing Planet: mars
5. Angels: Dominions
6. Chakras: Heart
7. Precious Stones: Jade
8. Tarot Card: Judgment
9. Candles: Pink
10. Oils: Bergamont Oil, Citronella Oil
11. Herbs: Master of the Woods, Lavender
12. Trees: Apple tree
13. Animal presence: Dog

THE SPELL

On a new moon lite a pink candle dress with bergamont oil and lavender. Place an image of a dog on the right side of the candle. On parchment paper write the name of the person you want forgiveness from, in dove's blood. Then place the name in a clear jar filled with a bed of master of the woods, sugar covered with rose petals.

INTENTION: TO BE ADMIRED

1. Moon Phase: Full Moon
2. Day of the week: Friday
3. Time of day: Evening
4. Governing Planet: Venus
5. Angels: Seraphim
6. Chakras: Crown
7. Precious Stones: Lapiz Lazuli
8. Tarot Card: Two of Cups
9. Candles: Purple
10. Oils: Allspice Oil, High John Oil
11. Herbs: Masters root, Five Finger Grass and Master of the Woods
12. Trees: Apple Tree
13. Animal presence: Cat, Crow

THE SPELL

On the night of a full moon lite a candle dressed with all spice and high john oil sprinkle with master of the woods. In a small green flannel bag carry it with you for nine days masters root, five-finger grass anointed with allspice oil.

INTENTION: GAIN MOTHER INLAWS LOVE

1. Moon Phase: Full Moon
2. Day of the week: Friday
3. Time of day: Evening
4. Governing Planet: Venus
5. Angels: Dominion
6. Chakras: Heart
7. Precious Stones: Onyx
8. Tarot Card: Two of Pentacles
9. Candles: Red, Pink
10. Oils: Bergamont Oil, Patchouli Oil
11. Herbs: Star Anise, Violet Leaf, Gilead Buds and Damiana
12. Trees: Palm Tree
13. Animal presence: Humming Bird

THE SPELL

On the night of a full moon lite a red and pink candle dress with one drop of bergamont and one drop of patchouli sprinkle damiana. In a clear jar add half sugar gilead buds and violet leaf. On parchment paper in dove's blood write your mother in laws name along with your name and cover with honey then place deep within the sugar jar. Keep under your bed for 21 days for remarkable results on the next full moon.

INTENTION: GET YOUR LOVER BACK

1. Moon Phase: Full Moon
2. Day of the week: Friday
3. Time of day: Evening
4. Governing Planet: Venus
5. Angels: Dominion
6. Chakras: Heart
7. Precious Stones: Onyx
8. Tarot Card: Two of Pentacles
9. Candles: Red, Pink
10. Oils: Bergamont Oil, Patchouli Oil
11. Herbs: Star Anise, Violet Leaf, Gilead Buds and Damiana
12. Trees: Palm Tree
13. Animal presence: Humming Bird

THE SPELL

On a full moon lite a pink and red candle dressed with patchouli and violet leaf. Write your lovers initials on the candles. Place the two of pentacles in the middle of both candles. You will need your lover's undergarment and red ribbon. In the center of the undergarment saturate with nine drops of bergamont, nine drops of patchouli add star anise, gilead buds and damiana. Fold the undergarment towards you then wrap two times and tie one knot. Place under your pillow for nine days.

INTENTION: GET RID OF AN UNWANTED LOVER

1. Moon Phase: Waning Moon
2. Day of the week: Tuesday
3. Time of day: Evening
4. Governing Planet: Mars
5. Angels: Thrones
6. Chakras: Root
7. Precious Stones: Onyx
8. Tarot Card: Death
9. Candles: Black
10. Oils: Garlic oil, Rattlesnake root oil
11. Herbs: Rattlesnake, Cherry Bark, and Coriander
12. Trees: Cherry Tree
13. Animal presence: Vulture

THE SPELL

On a waning moon, light a black candle dressed with rattlesnake oil sprinkle coriander. Place the death card in front of the candle. Gather all pictures and belongings of the lover along with nail clippings and or strands of hair. Go outdoors and start a fire adding rattlesnake root and cherry bark over all the belongings before throwing them in the fire. Allow the fire to completely consume all items. The unwanted lover will leave you alone for good.

INTENTION: GET THE JUDGE ON YOUR SIDE

1. Moon Phase: Full Moon
2. Day of the week: Wednesday
3. Time of day: Evening
4. Governing Planet: Mercury
5. Angels: Thrones
6. Chakras: Throat
7. Precious Stones: Onyx
8. Tarot Card: Justice Card
9. Candles: Brown
10. Oils: Marjoram Oil
11. Herbs: Sumac Berry, calendula
12. Trees: Oak Tree
13. Animal presence: Owl

THE SPELL

On the night of a full moon write the name of the judge in virgin parchment paper in dove's blood ink anoint with marjoram oil. Drop the name into a jar of damnation water with a handful of sumac berry add the onyx stone over the name and keep it there for nine days. Carry calendula on you the day of the court. The judge will see it your way.

INTENTION: GET YOUR LOVER TO CALL

1. Moon Phase: Full Moon
2. Day of the week: Friday
3. Time of day: Evening
4. Governing Planet: Venus
5. Angels: Dominion
6. Chakras: Heart
7. Precious Stones: Onyx
8. Tarot Card: Tow of Wands
9. Candles: Red
10. Oils: Bergamont Oil, Rose Oil
11. Herbs: Star Anise, Tobacco, and Violet Leaf
12. Trees: Apple Tree
13. Animal presence: Humming Bird

THE SPELL

On a full moon lite a red candle dressed with bergamont oil. On an image of a humming bird add rose oil and star anise place it in a white envelope and sleep under it for three nights, your lover will call out of the blue.

INTENTION: GAIN POWER

1. Moon Phase: Waxing Moon
2. Day of the week: Thursday
3. Time of day: Evening
4. Governing Planet: Jupiter
5. Angels: Seraphim
6. Chakras: Crown
7. Precious Stones: Lapiz Lazuli, Emerald
8. Tarot Card: King of Swords
9. Candles: Yellow, Purple
10. Oils: Bergamont, Calamus Oil, High John Oil
11. Herbs: Calamus root, Five Finger Root and Master of the Woods
12. Trees: Oak Tree
13. Animal presence: Bald Eagle, Horse

THE SPELL

On a waxing moon, light a yellow and purple candle dressed with high john oil and five-finger root. Then make a circle on the North side of your home of oak tree leaves on the ground filled with master of the woods and sprinkle calamus root. Stand in the center with the king of swords card in your right hand and a lapis lazuli on your left.

INTENTION: DOMINATE YOUR BOSS

1. Moon Phase: Full Moon
2. Day of the week: Saturday
3. Time of day: Evening
4. Governing Planet: Saturn
5. Angels: Seraphim
6. Chakras: Crown
7. Precious Stones: Lapiz Lazuli
8. Tarot Card: Magician
9. Candles: Black
10. Oils: Beramont Oil, Controlling Oil and Bend Over oil
11. Herbs: Quassia Chips, Devils shoe string
12. Trees: Oak Tree
13. Animal presence: Red Tail Hawk

THE SPELL

On a full moon lite a black candle write your bosses name backwards on parchment paper in dragons blood saturate with controlling oil and bend over oil. Then crush the paper and wrap it with black yarn away from you until you build a ball. Then bury the ball with devils shoestring over it.

INTENTION: NEW CAREER

1. Moon Phase: Full Moon
2. Day of the week: Thursday
3. Time of day: Evening
4. Governing Planet: Jupiter
5. Angels: Gabriel
6. Chakras: Third Eye
7. Precious Stones: Malachite
8. Tarot Card: Ace of Wands
9. Candles: Orange
10. Oils: Allspice Oil
11. Herbs: Solomon's seal root, Queen of the Meadow, Fenugreek
12. Trees: Palm Tree
13. Animal presence: Fox

THE SPELL

On the night of a full moon light an orange candle saturated with allspice oil. On parchment paper write the name of the new career you wish to have with your name alongside it in dove's blood, place it under the ace of wands card. As you look into the flame envision yourself having the new career. Then run the bath water adding queen of the meadow and soak for thirty-six minutes, you will be in the new career by next full moon.

INTENTION: GET A LOAN

1. Moon Phase: Waxing Moon
2. Day of the week: Thursday
3. Time of day: Evening
4. Governing Planet: Jupiter
5. Angels: Gabriel
6. Chakras: Solar Plexus
7. Precious Stones: Onyx
8. Tarot Card: Ten of Cups
9. Candles: Green
10. Oils: Allspice oil, Nutmeg oil
11. Herbs: Alfalfa, mandrake root
12. Trees: Palm Tree
13. Animal presence: Spider, Grasshopper

THE SPELL

On a night of a waxing moon, light a green candle dressed with nutmeg oil, allspice oil sprinkling mandrake root on it. Place the ten of cups on the right side of the candle. As you look at the flame call upon spider presence to capture in its web your new loan. Place a twenty-dollar bill around your photograph and carry it with you when you apply for the loan.

INTENTION: DEVELOP PERSONAL POWER

1. Moon Phase: Waxing Moon
2. Day of the week: Sunday
3. Time of day: Evening
4. Governing Planet: The sun
5. Angels: Seraphim
6. Chakras: Throat
7. Precious Stones: Gold
8. Tarot Card: Two of Pentacles
9. Candles: Gold
10. Oils: Sage oil
11. Herbs: Acacia Leaf, Golden Seal Root and Burning Bush
12. Trees: Oak tree
13. Animal presence: Hawk

THE SPELL

On a waxing moon, light a gold candle dressed in sage oil. Place an image of a hawk on the right side of the candle with golden seal root on top of it. On the left side place the two of pentacles. Invoke Seraphim, the most highly regarded angel to gain access to greater knowledge that will lead you to expand your personal power. Carry with you in a satchel burning bush for 21 days and feel your personal power increase exponentially.

INTENTION: TO RECEIVE GOOD GRADES

1. Moon Phase: Waxing Moon
2. Day of the week: Wednesday
3. Time of day: Evening
4. Governing Planet: Mercury
5. Angels: Cherubim
6. Chakras: Crown
7. Precious Stones: Sodalite
8. Tarot Card: Eight of Wands
9. Candles: Purple
10. Oils: Amber Oil, High John Oil
11. Herbs: peach Tree Leaves, Wintergreen
12. Trees: Oak Tree
13. Animal presence: Panther

THE SPELL

On a waxing moon, light a purple candle dressed with amber oil and wintergreen. On parchment paper write your name along with a big letter A and saturate it with high john oil and two peach tree leaves place the A on the eight of wands. Place it where you study, see your grades rise.

INTENTION: TO GRADUATE

1. Moon Phase: Full Moon
2. Day of the week: Saturday
3. Time of day: Evening
4. Governing Planet: Saturn
5. Angels: Cherubim
6. Chakras: Crown
7. Precious Stones: Sodalite, Lapiz Lazuli
8. Tarot Card: World
9. Candles: Purple, White
10. Oils: Allspice Oil
11. Herbs: Solomon's seal root, Five Finger Grass and Master root
12. Trees: Palm Tree
13. Animal presence: Crow, Hawk

THE SPELL

On the first day of the full moon, light a white and purple candle dress with allspice and Solomon's seal. Then anoint a lapis lazuli stone with allspice oil and master root to be carried with you for nine days. Go to the nearest steps, as you walk up the stairs see yourself getting closer to graduation, at the top of the stairs lift up both candles up in the air simultaneously see your self graduating.

INTENTION: TELEPATIC MESSAGE

1. Moon Phase: Waxing Moon
2. Day of the week: Friday
3. Time of day: Evening
4. Governing Planet: Venus
5. Angels: Thrones
6. Chakras: Throat
7. Precious Stones: Tanzanite
8. Tarot Card: Ten of Swords
9. Candles: White
10. Oils: Orange Oil, Rosemary oil
11. Herbs: Tobacco, Dill seed
12. Trees: Elder
13. Animal presence: Duck, Humming Bird

THE SPELL

On a waxing moon or whenever you want to send someone a message, go to your altar light a white candle dressed with orange oil and dill seeds. Then look into the candle flame when relaxed place two drops of rosemary oil on your hands rub them together, now place your hands in the prayer position and think of the person you want to send a message to. When you have a clear image of the person move your hands in opposite directions say their name then tell them your message, bring your hands together and release them in upward motion.

INTENTION: TRAVEL BY CRUISELINER

1. Moon Phase: Full Moon
2. Day of the week: Monday
3. Time of day: Evening
4. Governing Planet: Moon
5. Angels: Cherubim
6. Chakras: Crown
7. Precious Stones: Lapiz Lazuli, Coral
8. Tarot Card: World
9. Candles: Blue
10. Oils: High John oil, Ginseng oil
11. Herbs: Master of the Woods, Solomon's seal root
12. Trees: Apple Tree
13. Animal presence: Falcon

THE SPELL

On the darkest night of a full moon light a blue candle dressed with Ginseng oil sprinkle with Solomon's seal root. Envision the falcon presence in the direction you wish to travel to. On your alter make a small bed of apple tree leaves and place a small model ship of a cruise liner on top and anoint every night for nine days, you will travel shortly.

INTENTION: TRAVEL BY AIR

1. Moon Phase: Full Moon
2. Day of the week: Monday
3. Time of day: Evening
4. Governing Planet: Moon
5. Angels: Cherubim
6. Chakras: Crown
7. Precious Stones: Lapiz Lazuli, Coral
8. Tarot Card: World
9. Candles: Silver
10. Oils: High John Oil,
11. Herbs: Master of the Woods, Solomon's seal root
12. Trees: Birch Tree
13. Animal presence: Falcon

THE SPELL

On the darkest night of a full moon light a silver candle dressed with High john oil sprinkled with Solomon's seal. Stare at the flame envision the falcon presence flying next to you on the plane and making a connection with the falcon. On your alter make a small bed of Birch Tree leaves and place a small model of a plane on top and anoint every night for nine days, you will travel by plane soon.

INTENTION: TRAVEL SHORT JOURNEYS

1. Moon Phase: Full Moon
2. Day of the week: Monday
3. Time of day: Evening
4. Governing Planet: Moon
5. Angels: Cherubim
6. Chakras: Crown
7. Precious Stones: Lapiz Lazuli, Coral
8. Tarot Card: World
9. Candles: Gold, Purple
10. Oils: High John oil, Ginseng oil
11. Herbs: Master of the Woods, Solomon's seal root
12. Trees: Apple Tree
13. Animal presence: Falcon

THE SPELL

On the darkest night of a full moon light a gold candle and add nine drops of Ginseng, High John oil sprinkle with Solomon's seal root and Master of the woods. Place the world card in front of the candle. Envision the falcon and say out loud North, South, East and West stand up and spin your body around once. Then take a suitcase anointed with High John oil outside your door, with a big smile on your face repeat four times for each direction, you will travel soon after.

INTENTION: WORLD TRAVEL

1. Moon Phase: Full Moon
2. Day of the week: Monday
3. Time of day: Evening
4. Governing Planet: Moon
5. Angels: Cherubim
6. Chakras: Crown
7. Precious Stones: Lapiz Lazuli, Coral
8. Tarot Card: World
9. Candles: Gold, Purple
10. Oils: High John oil, Ginseng oil
11. Herbs: Master of the Woods, Solomon's seal root
12. Trees: Apple Tree
13. Animal presence: Falcon

THE SPELL

On the darkest night of a full moon light a gold candle and add nine drops of Ginseng, High John oil sprinkle with Solomon's seal root and Master of the woods. Place the world card in front of the candle. Envision the falcon and say out loud North, South, East and West stand up and spin your body around once. Then take a suitcase anointed with High John oil outside your door, with a big smile on your face repeat four times for each direction, you will travel soon after.

INTENTION: HEALTH

1. Moon Phase: Waxing Moon
2. Day of the week: Sunday
3. Time of day: Evening
4. Governing Planet: The Sun
5. Angels: Cherubim
6. Chakras: Crown
7. Precious Stones: Lapiz Lazuli
8. Tarot Card: World
9. Candles: White
10. Oils: Van-Van oil, High John Oil
11. Herbs: Mugwort, Safflower
12. Trees: Apple Tree
13. Animal presence: Falcon

THE SPELL

On a Sunday Morning use the power of the sun to strengthen your body to better health. Lite a white candle dressed with van van oil, safflower and mugwort. As you stare into the flame see yourself healthy draw health towards you. Write your full name on parchment paper in dove's ink with the word healthy under your name, tip the candle dropping wax on your name then white envelope place your name inside and seal it with wax. Place it under your pillow sleep on it for nine consecutive nights. Let the candle burn out on its own by the time the moon is new your health will return.

INTENTION: HEAL THE BODY

1. Moon Phase: Waxing Moon
2. Day of the week: Sunday
3. Time of day: Morning
4. Governing Planet: Sun
5. Angels: Raphael
6. Chakras: Sacral
7. Precious Stones: Crystal, Ruby
8. Tarot Card: Three of Pentacles
9. Candles: Blue
10. Oils: Camphor Oil
11. Herbs: Sarsparilla, All Heal Leaves, Althaea Leaves, Asafoetida
12. Trees: Cedar
13. Animal presence: Eagle, Dog

THE SPELL

On a waxing moon lite a blue candle dressed with camphor oil and sarparilla. Place the three of pentacles on the right side of the candle. Stare at the flame and see yourself healthy moving dancing. In a gold small bag place a crystal anointed with camphor oil and mixture of sarparilla, all heal leaves; althaea leaves carry it with you for nine days.

INTENTION: HEAL THE MIND

1. Moon Phase: Waxing Moon
2. Day of the week: Sunday
3. Time of day: Morning
4. Governing Planet: Sun
5. Angels: Raphael
6. Chakras: Solar Plexus
7. Precious Stones: Amethyst, Agate
8. Tarot Card: Moon
9. Candles: Blue
10. Oils: Bay Leaf Oil, Camphor Oil
11. Herbs: Betony
12. Trees: Cedar
13. Animal presence: Panther

THE SPELL

On a waxing moon lite a blue candle dressed with bay leaf oil and althaea leaves. Place the moon card on the right side of the candle. Stare at the flame and allow your mind to be blank. In a blue small bag place amethyst anointed with camphor oil and betony carry it with you for three days.

INTENTION: DISTANCE HEALING

1. Moon Phase: Waning Moon
2. Day of the week: Sunday
3. Time of day: Morning
4. Governing Planet: Sun
5. Angels: Raphael
6. Chakras: Solar Plexus
7. Precious Stones: Crystal, Apatite and Amber
8. Tarot Card: Three of Pentacles
9. Candles: Blue, White
10. Oils: Camphor Oil
11. Herbs: Sarsparilla, Thyme and Boneset
12. Trees: Cedar
13. Animal presence: Cat

THE SPELL

On a waning moon go to your altar light a white candle dressed with camphor oil and Thyme. Then stare at the flame and call upon the cat presence then see the image of the person clearly, now mentally place a white light from the bottom of their feet to the top of the head then add a gold light above the head and see their body absorbing the golden light.

INTENTION: REMOVE DEPRESSION

1. Moon Phase: Waning Moon
2. Day of the week: Tuesday
3. Time of day: Morning
4. Governing Planet: Mars
5. Angels: Raphael
6. Chakras: Solar Plexus
7. Precious Stones: Amethyst, Copper
8. Tarot Card: Two of Cups
9. Candles: Black
10. Oils: Bay Leaf Oil
11. Herbs: Coltsfoot, Blacksnake root
12. Trees: Ash Tree
13. Animal presence: Spider

THE SPELL

On a waning moon light a black candle dressed with bay leaf oil sprinkled with coltsfoot. On your altar make a bed of ash leaves and place the two of cups in front of the candle. Then run a bath with warm water adding a handful of bay leaves to the water. Soak in the bathe for twenty-nine minutes. Then chew a bit of blacksnake root your depression will wane with the moon.

INTENTION: REMOVE BAD HABITS

1. Moon Phase: Waning Moon
2. Day of the week: Tuesday
3. Time of day: Morning
4. Governing Planet: Mars
5. Angels: Raphael
6. Chakras: Solar Plexus
7. Precious Stones: Aventurine, Copper
8. Tarot Card: Ace of Pentacles
9. Candles: Black
10. Oils: Basil Oil
11. Herbs: Sage
12. Trees: Ash Tree
13. Animal presence: Vulture

THE SPELL

On a waning moon lite a black candle dressed with basil oil place the ace of pentacles on the left side of the candle and sprinkled with sage. Then write your bad habits in black ink on bay leaves take the leaves to fast moving water and release them. The bad habits will leave your life.

INTENTION: REPEL NIGHTMARES

1. Moon Phase: Waning Moon
2. Day of the week: Tuesday
3. Time of day: Morning
4. Governing Planet: Mars
5. Angels: Raphael
6. Chakras: Solar Lexus
7. Precious Stones: Obsidian
8. Tarot Card: Four of Swords
9. Candles: Black
10. Oils: Basil Oil, Camphor Oil
11. Herbs: Thyme, Pine Needles
12. Trees: Bonsai
13. Animal presence: Wolf, Hawk

THE SPELL

On the night of a waning moon, light a black candle make a triangle with the pine needles and sprinkle thyme over it, then keep an image of a hawk or wolf anointed with basil oil and camphor oil over your bed.

INTENTION: TO SUMMON THE ANGELS

1. Moon Phase: Full Moon
2. Day of the week: Wednesday
3. Time of day: Evening
4. Governing Planet: Mercury
5. Angels: Cherubim
6. Chakras: Solar Plexus
7. Precious Stones: Crystal, Tanzanite
8. Tarot Card: Hierophant
9. Candles: Blue
10. Oils: Myrrh Oil,
11. Herbs: Frankincense, Anise seeds
12. Trees: Elder
13. Animal presence: Red Tail Hawk, Eagle

THE SPELL

On a full moon light three white candles dressed with myrrh oil add one anise seed per candle then place over a bed of elder. Light frankincense incense and call out to the angels by name, stare at the flame to quite the mind to be open to receive.

INTENTION: TO END A RELATIONSHIP

1. Moon Phase: Waning Moon
2. Day of the week: Tuesday
3. Time of day: Evening
4. Governing Planet: Mars
5. Angels: Thrones
6. Chakras: Throat
7. Precious Stones: Tiger Eye
8. Tarot Card: Death Card
9. Candles: Black
10. Oils: Lotus Oil, Lemon Oil
11. Herbs: Lemon Verbena, Alkanet root, and Guinea Pepper
12. Trees: Birch
13. Animal presence: Panther, Skunk

THE SPELL

On the night of a waning moon, Light a black candle dress with lemon oil and sprinkle guinea pepper. On parchment paper in dragon's blood write the name backwards of the person you want out of your life sprinkle guinea pepper and lemon oil. Place over the death card. Go to a nearby river and fold the name away from you then release it into the river. The relationship will end quickly.

INTENTION: TO END HOSTILITY IN THE HOME

1. Moon Phase: Waning Moon
2. Day of the week: Tuesday
3. Time of day: Morning
4. Governing Planet: Mars
5. Angels: Thrones
6. Chakras: Root
7. Precious Stones: Jade
8. Tarot Card: Ten of swords
9. Candles: Blue
10. Oils: Basil Oil
11. Herbs: Althaea Root, Lemon Mint, and Pennyroyal
12. Trees: Bonsai
13. Animal presence: Wolf

THE SPELL

On a waning moon, light a Blue candle dress with basil oil sprinkle pennyroyal. Place the ten of swords on the right side of the candle. Plant a bonsai plant on the right side of the house add a handful of Althea root to the base of the plant, hostility will end quickly.

INTENTION: SAVE YOUR MARRIAGE

1. Moon Phase: Full Moon
2. Day of the week: Friday
3. Time of day: Evening
4. Governing Planet: Venus
5. Angels: Dominion
6. Chakras: Heart
7. Precious Stones: Opal
8. Tarot Card: Four of Wands
9. Candles: White, Red
10. Oils: Cardamom Oil
11. Herbs: Red Clover Flower, Pennyroyal, and Periwinkle
12. Trees: Apple Tree
13. Animal presence: Fox

THE SPELL

On the night of a full moon light a white and red candle dressed with cardamom oil sprinkled with red clover flower. Place an opal stone on the right side of the candle sprinkle with periwinkle. Take a picture of yourself and of your spouse place one card on top of the others with the eyes looking at each other. Keep in a safe secret place on a bed of apple tree leaves.

INTENTION: AWAKEN PSYCHIC VISIONS

1. Moon Phase: Full Moon
2. Day of the week: Monday
3. Time of day: Evening
4. Governing Planet: Moon
5. Angels: Thrones
6. Chakras: Third Eye
7. Precious Stones: Azurite, Crystals and Citrine
8. Tarot Card: Moon
9. Candles: Blue
10. Oils: Anise Oil, Jasmine Oil
11. Herbs: Star Anise, Saffron, Sandalwood, and yarrow Flower
12. Trees: Banyan, Elder
13. Animal presence: Bald Eagle, Elephant

THE SPELL

On the night of a full moon in your backyard light a fire in a pit, then add a handful of salt into the fire this will turn the red flame blue, then burn anise seeds, yarrow flower and saffron. As the flames in the fire turns blue stare into the fire to be open to receive visions.

INTENTION: INCREASE MENTAL POWERS

1. Moon Phase: Full Moon
2. Day of the week: Thursday
3. Time of day: Evening
4. Governing Planet: Jupiter
5. Angels: Seraphim
6. Chakras: Crown
7. Precious Stones: Golden Beryl
8. Tarot Card: Moon
9. Candles: Silver
10. Oils: Frankincense Oil, Bergamont Oil
11. Herbs: Blood Root, Pepper Tree Leaves, and Agrimony
12. Trees: Oak Tree
13. Animal presence: Crow, Red Tailed Hawk

THE SPELL

On the night of a full moon light a silver candle dressed with bergamont oil sprinkled with Blood root. Place the moon card on the right side of the candle with a golden beryl on top. Carry with you a crow feather anointed with frankincense for nine days.

INTENTION: TO CALL UPON ANCESTORS

1. Moon Phase: Full Moon
2. Day of the week: Wednesday
3. Time of day: Evening
4. Governing Planet: Mercury
5. Angels: Seraphim
6. Chakras: Crown
7. Precious Stones: Crystal, Tanzanite
8. Tarot Card: High Priestess
9. Candles: Blue, White
10. Oils: Myrrh Oil, Jasmine Oil
11. Herbs: Wormwood
12. Trees: Beech
13. Animal presence: Bald Eagle, Red Tail Hawk

THE SPELL

On the night of a full moon light a blue candle dress with myrrh oil and white candle dress with jasmine oil. Stare into the flame as you do see a white light entering your body from your feet upwards to your head then place a golden light above your head and allow that light energy to penetrate your body. Pick up the high priestess card and place between your palms, call out to your ancestors in your mind keep your mind blank to receive the message.

INTENTION: TO RECEIVE ANCIENT KNOWLEDGE

1. Moon Phase: Full Moon
2. Day of the week: Wednesday
3. Time of day: Evening
4. Governing Planet: Mercury
5. Angels: Seraphim
6. Chakras: Crown
7. Precious Stones: Crystal, Tanzanite
8. Tarot Card: High Priestess
9. Candles: White
10. Oils: Myrrh Oil, Frankincense Oil
11. Herbs: Solomon's seal root, Sage smudge stick
12. Trees: Beech
13. Animal presence: Bald Eagle, Elephant and Whale

THE SPELL

On a full moon light a white candle and place a white circle of powder or salt on the floor. Place Solomon's seal roots in the center of the circle. Rub myrrh oil and frankincense oil to your hands and sit in the circle. Light a sage smudge stick and call upon the spirit you wish to contact. Quiet the mind to receive wisdom.

INTENTION: MAKE CONTACT WITH THE DEPARTED

1. Moon Phase: Full Moon
2. Day of the week: Saturday
3. Time of day: Evening
4. Governing Planet: Saturn
5. Angels: Cherubim
6. Chakras: Third eye
7. Precious Stones: Crystal, Tanzanite
8. Tarot Card: Death
9. Candles: White
10. Oils: Anise Oil
11. Herbs: Star Anise, Absinthe
12. Trees: Beech
13. Animal presence: Red Tail Hawk, Ghost Owl

THE SPELL

On the night of a full moon light a white candle dress with anise place the death card in front of the candle. Burn star anise and absinthe once the incense surrounds you call out for a sign of the person you wish to contact.

INTENTION: ATTRACT MONEY

1. Moon Phase: Waxing moon
2. Day of the week: Thursday
3. Time of day: Evening
4. Governing Planet: Jupiter
5. Angels: Gabriel
6. Chakras: Throat
7. Precious Stones: Onyx, Jade, and Emerald
8. Tarot Card: Queen of Pentacles
9. Candles: Green, Yellow
10. Oils: Allspice oil, Patchouli oil
11. Herbs: Wintergreen, Bayberry Root, and Snake Lily
12. Trees: Palm Tree
13. Animal presence: Grasshopper

THE SPELL

On a waxing moon, light a green candle dress it with allspice and patchouli carve the amount of money you desire on the candle. Place the queen of pentacles in front of the candle on top of palm tree leaves with a jade stone on it. As you watch the flame envision the angel Gabriel assisting you in receiving money into your home. Place a mat in private, inside of your front door with wintergreen, bayberry root and a twenty-dollar bill under your mat, as you step on it every day the money rolls in.

INTENTION: STEADY WORK

1. Moon Phase: Full Moon
2. Day of the week: Saturday
3. Time of day: Evening
4. Governing Planet: Saturn
5. Angels: Gabriel
6. Chakras: Root
7. Precious Stones: Turquoise
8. Tarot Card: Four of Pentacles
9. Candles: Green
10. Oils: Allspice Oil, Bay Berry Oil
11. Herbs: Allspice Berries, Asafoetida
12. Trees: Bonsai
13. Animal presence: Dog

THE SPELL

On a full moon, anoint your hands with allspice berries and bay berry oil then plant an onion bulb with the name of the company you work for on the North side of your home. Every time you look in the direction of the bulb will remind you of the anchor you have for steady work. Water for nine days consecutively, then as needed. This is a powerful you could be promoted.

INTENTION: ATTRACT GOOD BUSINESS PARTNERS

1. Moon Phase: Waxing Moon
2. Day of the week: Saturday
3. Time of day: Morning
4. Governing Planet: Saturday
5. Angels: Gabriel
6. Chakras: Solar Lexus
7. Precious Stones: Aqua Marine, Emeralds
8. Tarot Card: Three of Cups
9. Candles: Orange, Green
10. Oils: Allspice Oil, Patchouli Oil
11. Herbs: Solomon's seal root, Allspice Berries, and Cloves
12. Trees: Palm Tree
13. Animal presence: Fox

THE SPELL

On a Saturday morning place two palm tree leaves with the leaves intertwined with each other on the physical business turn on a green and orange candle anointed with 1 drop of allspice and 1 drop of patchouli oil per candle let them burn. Visualize the right business partners coming to you.

INTENTION: SHED YOUR PROBLEMS

1. Moon Phase: Waning Moon
2. Day of the week: Sunday
3. Time of day: Evening
4. Governing Planet: Sun
5. Angels: Michael
6. Chakras: Crown
7. Precious Stones: Agate
8. Tarot Card: Ten of Swords
9. Candles: Black
10. Oils: Lemon Grass Oil
11. Herbs: Hyssop
12. Trees: Birch
13. Animal presence: Panther

THE SPELL

On a waning moon place a black candle dress with lemon grass oil sprinkle with hyssop. On parchment paper write the problem you wish to shed place under the candle. Keep it there until the candle burns out then throw it in an open fire, your problem will dissipate.

INTENTION: ETERNAL YOUTH

1. Moon Phase: Waxing Moon
2. Day of the week: Friday
3. Time of day: Morning
4. Governing Planet: Venus
5. Angels: Raphael
6. Chakras:
7. Precious Stones: Morganite
8. Tarot Card: Page of Cups
9. Candles: Pink
10. Oils: Lavender Oil,
11. Herbs: Angelica
12. Trees: Palm Tree
13. Animal presence: Crow

THE SPELL

On a waxing moon light a pink candle dress with lavender oil. Place a bed of palm trees on your altar placing the page of cups on top. Stare into the flame and picture a happy time in your life. At this moment chew a bit of angelica it will maintain your youthfulness and prolongs life.

INTENTION: LOOSE WEIGHT

1. Moon Phase: Waning Moon
2. Day of the week: Sunday
3. Time of day: Morning
4. Governing Planet: Sun
5. Angels: Michael
6. Chakras: Solar Plexus
7. Precious Stones: Morganite, Rose Quartz
8. Tarot Card: Eight of Pentacles
9. Candles: Black, Purple
10. Oils: frankincense
11. Herbs: Lemon herb
12. Trees: Palm Tree
13. Animal presence: Humming Bird

THE SPELL

On a full moon place your photograph on a palm tree leaves place in your closet sprinkle lemon herb on the bed of the palm tree once a week light a black candle anointed with frankincense.

INTENTION: ATTRACT A WEALTHY LOVER

1. Moon Phase: Full Moon
2. Day of the week: Thursday
3. Time of day: Midnight
4. Governing Planet: Jupiter
5. Angels: Seraphim
6. Chakras: Crown
7. Precious Stones: Aqua Aura, Lodestone
8. Tarot Card: Nine of Pentacles
9. Candles: Yellow
10. Oils: High John Oil, Allspice Oil and Lavender
11. Herbs: Solomon Seal, Jezebel Root
12. Trees: Oak Tree
13. Animal presence: Rabbit, Humming Bird

THE SPELL

On a full moon light a yellow candle. In a small green flannel bag carry Solomon's seal, Jezebel root and lavender. Then place a lodestone anointed with high john oil and allspice oil. Carry it with you at all times.

INTENTION: NEW YEAR SPELL

1. Moon Phase: Full Moon
2. Day of the week: Tuesday
3. Time of day: Evening
4. Governing Planet: Mars
5. Angels: Seraphim
6. Chakras: Crown
7. Precious Stones: Amethyst
8. Tarot Card: Moon
9. Candles: White
10. Oils: Holy oil
11. Herbs: Rosemary, Sage
12. Trees: Oak Tree
13. Animal presence: Red tailed Hawk

THE SPELL

On New Years evening light twelve white candles dressed in holy oil and rosemary. Place them in a circle then add the moon card in the center of the candles. Envision the presence of the red tailed hawk and place a lapis lazuli stone on top of the card. Then light a sage smudge stick and smudge yourself beginning with your feet upwards toward your head. Then smudge each of the twelve candles saying out loud what you desire to achieve that month and so fourth.

BLACK MAGIC SPELLS

INTENTION: GET RID OF AN UNWANTED LOVER

1. Moon Phase: Waning Moon
2. Day of the week: Tuesday
3. Time of day: Evening
4. Governing Planet: Mars
5. Angels: Thrones
6. Chakras: Root
7. Precious Stones: Onyx
8. Tarot Card: Death
9. Candles: Black
10. Oils: Garlic oil, Rattlesnake root oil
11. Herbs: Rattlesnake, Cherry Bark, and Coriander
12. Trees: Cherry Tree
13. Animal presence: Vulture

THE SPELL

On a waning moon, light a black candle dressed with rattlesnake oil sprinkle coriander. Place the death card in front of the candle. Gather all pictures and belongings of the lover along with nail clippings and or strands of hair. Go outdoors and start a fire adding rattlesnake root and cherry bark over all the belongings before throwing them in the fire. Allow the fire to completely consume all items. The unwanted lover will leave you alone for good.

INTENTION: SEPARATE LOVERS

1. Moon Phase: Waning Moon
2. Day of the week: Saturday
3. Time of day: Evening
4. Governing Planet: Saturn
5. Angels: Seraphim
6. Chakras: Crown
7. Precious Stones: Onyx
8. Tarot Card: Death Card
9. Candles: Black
10. Oils: Red Pepper Oil, Bitter Aloes Oil and Guinea Pepper Oil
11. Herbs: Lemon Verbena, Poppy Seed, Slippery Elm Walnut Leaf
12. Trees: Cherry Tree
13. Animal presence: Skunk, Bats

THE SPELL

On the night of a waning moon go to a secluded bridge light a black candle dressed with bitter aloes, lemon verbena and slippery elm. On parchment paper write the names of the lovers in dragons bold alongside each other sprinkle with a mixture of lemon verbena, poppy seed and walnut leaf then make a quick cut separating the names. Then bury one name on the right side of the bridge and the other name on the left side of the bridge. The lovers will separate quickly.

INTENTION: DISSOLVE A MARRIAGE

1. Moon Phase: Waning Moon
2. Day of the week: Saturday
3. Time of day: Evening
4. Governing Planet: Saturn
5. Angels: Seraphim
6. Chakras: Crown
7. Precious Stones: Onyx
8. Tarot Card: Death Card
9. Candles: Black
10. Oils: Red Pepper Oil, Bitter Aloes Oil and Guinea Pepper Oil
11. Herbs: Lemon Verbena, Poppy Seed, Slippery Elm, Pepper
12. Trees: Cherry Tree
13. Animal presence: Skunk, Bats

THE SPELL

On a waning moon, light a black candle dressed with red pepper oil and poppy seed. At a secluded bridge with fast moving water write on parchment paper the names of the couple sprinkle with lemon verbena then separate the names with one clean cut. Bury the names on opposite sides. On the third night go to the bridge with the death card anointed with red, black pepper and bitter aloes. Release the card into fast moving water. The marriage will dissolve quickly.

INTENTION: HEX ENEMIES HOME

1. Moon Phase: Full Moon
2. Day of the week: Saturday
3. Time of day: Evening
4. Governing Planet: Saturn
5. Angels: Seraphim
6. Chakras: Crown
7. Precious Stones: Emerald
8. Tarot Card: Four of Pentacles turned upside down
9. Candles: Black
10. Oils: Myrrh Oil, Black Pepper Oil, and Vertivert
11. Herbs: Rue, Tila, Jezebel, Black Mustard Seed, and poppy seed
12. Trees: Cherry Tree
13. Animal presence: Horned Owl, Racoon

THE SPELL

On the night of a full moon conjure a mixture of black mustard seed, rue, tila and poppy seed anointed with vertivert oil. Go to the enemies home and place in the center of the home or property. Then anoint an image of a horned owl with black pepper oil and place where it will be found, the hex is complete.

INTENTION: HEX ENEMIES PERSONAL PROPERTY

1. Moon Phase: Full Moon
2. Day of the week: Saturday
3. Time of day: Evening
4. Governing Planet: Saturn
5. Angels: Seraphim
6. Chakras: Crown
7. Precious Stones: Emerald
8. Tarot Card: Seven of Wands
9. Candles: Black
10. Oils: Myrrh Oil, Black Pepper Oil
11. Herbs: Twitch's grass, Dog's Grass and Witch's Grass
12. Trees: Cherry Tree
13. Animal presence: Horned Owl, Raccoon

THE SPELL

On the evening of a full moon, mix myrrh oil, black pepper oil and witch's grass then anoint the personal property you desire to hex. The next time its used the hex will be cast.

INTENTION: HEX ENEMIES BUSINESS

1. Moon Phase: Full Moon
2. Day of the week: Saturday
3. Time of day: Evening
4. Governing Planet: Saturn
5. Angels: Seraphim
6. Chakras: Crown
7. Precious Stones: Emerald
8. Tarot Card: Four of Pentacles turned upside down
9. Candles: Black
10. Oils: Myrrh Oil, Black Pepper Oil, and Vertivert
11. Herbs: Rue, Tila, Jezebel Root and Black Mustard Seed
12. Trees: Cherry Tree
13. Animal presence: Horned Owl, Racoon

THE SPELL

On a full moon make a mixture of rue, tila, black mustard seed heavily anointed with black pepper oil make into a small ball then cover with black yarn to make into a ball. Go to the business and place it where it will not be easily seen it will fester and full power released when found.

INTENTION: DESTROY ENEMIES HARVEST

1. Moon Phase: Waning Moon
2. Day of the week: Wednesday
3. Time of day: Evening
4. Governing Planet: Mercury
5. Angels: Seraphim
6. Chakras: Crown
7. Precious Stones: Obsidian
8. Tarot Card: Seven of Pentacles turned upside down
9. Candles: Black
10. Oils: Garlic Clove Oil, Red Pepper Oil, Vertivert Oil
11. Herbs: Witch's Grass, Dog's Grass and Spanish moss
12. Trees: Cherry Tree
13. Animal presence: Horse, Wolf

THE SPELL

On midnight of a waning moon, light a black candle anointed with vertivert oil. Go to field place a handful of Witch's grass, dog's grass and Spanish moss to the four corners of the field. There will be no harvest

INTENTION: TO CHANGE YOUR ENEMIES MIND

1. Moon Phase: Full Moon
2. Day of the week: Tuesday
3. Time of day: Evening
4. Governing Planet: Mars
5. Angels: Seraphim
6. Chakras: Crown
7. Precious Stones: Amethyst
8. Tarot Card: Moon
9. Candles: Black
10. Oils: Controlling oil
11. Herbs: Licorice Root
12. Trees: Oak Tree
13. Animal presence: Raven, Owl

THE SPELL

On the evening of a full moon light a black candle dressed in controlling oil and licorice root then place the moon card in front of the candle. Envision the presence of the owl and place the amethyst stone on the left side of the candle, then see the face of your enemy, enter their mind and tell them what you want them to do. Your enemy will do your biding by the end of the third day of the dark moon.

INTENTION: COLLAPSE OF BUSINESS

1. Moon Phase: Waning Moon
2. Day of the week: Saturday
3. Time of day: Evening
4. Governing Planet: Saturn
5. Angels: Seraphim
6. Chakras: Crown
7. Precious Stones: Emerald
8. Tarot Card: Tower
9. Candles: Black
10. Oils: Poppy Seed Oil, Clove Oil, and Lemon Oil
11. Herbs: Tilia, Tormentilla, Twitch's Grass and Mustard seed
12. Trees: Cherry Tree
13. Animal presence: Red Tailed Fox

THE SPELL

On a waning moon, on parchment paper write the name of the business and owner backwards in dragon's blood anoint with poppy seed oil. Go to the cemetery take some graveyard dirt place in small box and the parchment paper cover with tormentila, tilia and witch's grass then seal with black candle drippings before burying it near the business.

INTENTION: REMOVAL OF FORTUNE

1. Moon Phase: Waning Moon
2. Day of the week: Saturday
3. Time of day: Midnight
4. Governing Planet: Saturn
5. Angels: Seraphim
6. Chakras: Crown
7. Precious Stones: Emerald
8. Tarot Card: Wheel Of Fortune turned upside down
9. Candles: Black
10. Oils: Guinea Pepper Oil, Cassia Oil and Lemon Oil
11. Herbs: Henbane, Rattlesnake Root, and Alkanet Root
12. Trees: Cherry Tree
13. Animal presence: Horned Owl

THE SPELL

On the night of a waning moon, light a black candle anointed with cassia oil with their name etched into the candle. Then sprinkle henbane, alkanet root in the perimeter of the enemy's home and place a handful of mustard seeds on the front door.

INTENTION: TO BE NAMED ON THE WILL

1. Moon Phase: Full Moon
2. Day of the week: Saturday
3. Time of day: Evening
4. Governing Planet: Saturday
5. Angels: Seraphim
6. Chakras: Crown
7. Precious Stones: Emerald
8. Tarot Card: Wheel of Fortune
9. Candles: Black and Orange
10. Oils: Garlic Oil, Guinea Pepper Oil, Rue oil and Rose oil
11. Herbs: Cinnamon, Rattle Snake Root, Witch's Grass, and Alkanet
12. Trees: Palm Tree
13. Animal presence: Owl, Bald Eagle

THE SPELL

On the night of a full moon light a black anoint with garlic oil, witch's grass and a orange candle anoint with rose oil then write your name in dove's blood alongside the name of the person's writing the will, then fold towards you. Place your names in a bed of rose petals and sugar to be kept in a clear jar, must be done nine days before the will is read each day sprinkle with cinnamon.

INTENTION: RETURN THE CURSE TO SENDER

1. Moon Phase: Full Moon
2. Day of the week: Saturday
3. Time of day: Evening
4. Governing Planet: Saturn
5. Angels: Michael
6. Chakras: Crown
7. Precious Stones:
8. Tarot Card: Sun turned upside down
9. Candles: Black
10. Oils: Blood root oil
11. Herbs: Blood Root, Pepper Tree Leaves, and Agrimony
12. Trees: Cherry Tree
13. Animal presence: Owl, Wolf

THE SPELL

On the night of a full moon light a black candle anointed with pepper leaves. Sprinkle bloodroots on the perimeter of your enemies home, then take a coconut make a small hole in it drain then refill with agrimony. Leave the coconut near their home cover with cherry tree leaves.

INTENTION: FORCE ENEMY TO MOVE AWAY

1. Moon Phase: Full Moon
2. Day of the week: Monday
3. Time of day: Evening
4. Governing Planet: Moon
5. Angels: Seraphim
6. Chakras: Crown
7. Precious Stones: Obsidian
8. Tarot Card: World card turned upside down
9. Candles: Black
10. Oils: Galangal Oil, Vertivert Oil
11. Herbs: Poke Root, Calamus root, and Cedar wood
12. Trees: Cypress
13. Animal presence: Skunk, Bat

THE SPELL

On the night of a full moon get a doll to represent the enemy take ninepins and poke them through in a straight line from the head down to the crotch area and leave them in. Anoint with vertivert oil and sprinkle Poke Root, Calamus Root and place on a bed of cypress in a small box. Take the box to a nearby river and release it, the enemy will move away quickly.

INTENTION: KEEP THE INLAWS AWAY

1. Moon Phase: Full Moon
2. Day of the week: Sunday
3. Time of day: Evening
4. Governing Planet: Sun
5. Angels: Seraphim
6. Chakras: Crown
7. Precious Stones: Sodalite
8. Tarot Card: Death Card
9. Candles: Black
10. Oils: Go away Oil, Bergamot Oil
11. Herbs: Oregano, Broom Straw, and Salt
12. Trees: Oak Tree
13. Animal presence: Red Tail Hawk

THE SPELL

On the night of a full moon, light a black candle anointed with bergamont oil and broom straw. Serve conjure of red pepper, black pepper and garlic as a condiment on a meal. As they leave your home throw salt outside your home.

A simple spell would be to write their names on parchment paper in dragon's blood on a full moon then go to a nearby river and watch as their names leaves your sight.

INTENTION: DESTROY ENEMY'S POWER

1. Moon Phase: Full Moon
2. Day of the week: Tuesday
3. Time of day: Evening
4. Governing Planet: Mars
5. Angels: Seraphim
6. Chakras: Crown
7. Precious Stones: Amber
8. Tarot Card: Two of Swords turned upside down
9. Candles: Black
10. Oils: Rue Oil, Black pepper Oil and Lemon Oil
11. Herbs: Poppy seed, Tilia, Vertivert, Knotweed, Black Mustard
12. Trees: Cherry Tree
13. Animal presence: Dragon Fly

THE SPELL

On a full moon, light a black candle anoint with black guinea pepper. Create a wax image of the enemy write their name into the wax, anoint with rue oil and lemon oil. Place one pin thru the head of the doll the other thru the heart and lay on a bed of devils shoestring then cover in black cloth and bury near a cemetery.

INTENTION: PREVENT ENEMY FROM TAKING ACTION

1. Moon Phase: Waning Moon
2. Day of the week: Monday
3. Time of day: Evening
4. Governing Planet: Moon
5. Angels: Seraphim
6. Chakras: Crown
7. Precious Stones: Flourite
8. Tarot Card: Eight of Swords
9. Candles: Black
10. Oils: Controlling Oil
11. Herbs: Hemlock, Twitch's grass, Valerian, and Vertivert
12. Trees: Cypress
13. Animal presence: Horned Owl

THE SPELL

On the night of a waning moon light a black candle with controlling oil. Get a picture of the enemy and sprinkle with hemlock, twitch's grass, valerian and vertivert. Go to the nearest cemetery and bury the picture. The enemy's ability to take action will cease.

INTENTION: SILENCE AN ENEMY

1. Moon Phase: Full Moon
2. Day of the week: Saturday
3. Time of day: Evening
4. Governing Planet: Saturn
5. Angels: Seraphim
6. Chakras: Crown
7. Precious Stones: Obsidian
8. Tarot Card: Hermit
9. Candles: Black
10. Oils: Black Mustard Oil, Myrrh Oil
11. Herbs: Knotweed, Sea Wrack, Vertivert and Barberry
12. Trees: Cherry tree
13. Animal presence: Red Tailed Hawk

THE SPELL

On the night of the full moon, light a black candle dress with vertivert, slippery elm and sea wrack. Then anoint a sharks tooth with myrrh oil sprinkled with knotweed and Barberry carry it with you in a red flannel bag to silence the enemy.

INTENTION: PREVENT SLEEP

1. Moon Phase: Full Moon
2. Day of the week: Saturday
3. Time of day: Evening
4. Governing Planet: Saturn
5. Angels: Seraphim
6. Chakras: Crown
7. Precious Stones: Obsidian
8. Tarot Card: Nine of swords
9. Candles: Black
10. Oils: Lemon Oil
11. Herbs: Valerian, Tormentilla, and Tila
12. Trees: Cherry Tree
13. Animal presence: Insects, Reptiles

THE SPELL

On the night of a full moon place an image of the enemy in a bed of valerian sprinkle tormentila and tila over it keep the image in a box where no light will enter it. The enemy will be unable to sleep.

INTENTION: REMOVE AN ENEMY FROM YOUR PATH

1. Moon Phase: Waning Moon
2. Day of the week: Saturday
3. Time of day: Evening
4. Governing Planet: Saturn
5. Angels: Seraphim
6. Chakras: Crown
7. Precious Stones: Amber
8. Tarot Card: Star turned upside down
9. Candles: Black
10. Oils: Vertivert Oil, Lemon Oil
11. Herbs: Guinea Pepper, Knotweed, and Barberry
12. Trees: Cypress
13. Animal presence: Horned Owl, Skunk

THE SPELL

On the night of a waning moon light a black candle as you anoint with vertivert oil envision skunk's presence repelling energy and see the enemy moving quickly away from you. Go to the enemy's home and place valerian and knotweed on the North side of the home. The enemy will no longer cross your path.

INTENTION: STRIKE DOWN THE ENEMY

1. Moon Phase: Full Moon
2. Day of the week: Saturday
3. Time of day: Evening
4. Governing Planet: Saturn
5. Angels: Seraphim
6. Chakras: Crown
7. Precious Stones: Obsidian
8. Tarot Card: Tower
9. Candles: Black
10. Oils: Guinea Pepper Oil, Black Mustard Seed Oil
11. Herbs: Vertivert, Valerian, and Knotweed
12. Trees: Cherry Tree
13. Animal presence: Horned Owl

THE SPELL

On a full moon make a doll of the enemy can be made of dough add guinea pepper oil and poppy seeds, vertivert and knotweed to the batch if you have a strand of hair or piece of clothing attach it to the doll. Then bury the doll near the cemetery with a black raven feather over it.

INTENTION: CAUSE ILLNESS

1. Moon Phase: Full Moon
2. Day of the week: Saturday
3. Time of day: Evening
4. Governing Planet: Saturn
5. Angels: Seraphim
6. Chakras: Crown
7. Precious Stones: Cinnabar
8. Tarot Card: Four of Swords turned upside down
9. Candles: Black
10. Oils: Asafoetida, Vandal root
11. Herbs: Patchouli, Mullein
12. Trees: Cypress
13. Animal presence: Insects, Crane

THE SPELL

On a full moon at midnight light a black candle dressed with pokeroot and patchouli oil. On parchment paper write their name backwards in dragon's blood. Mix into melted wax into a mixture of asafoetida, mullein and vandal root. Once hardened take the wax figure out to the moonlight and with your left hand crush the wax into pieces. The enemy will become ill quickly.

INTENTION: TO CAUSE DESPAIR

1. Moon Phase: Full Moon
2. Day of the week: Tuesday
3. Time of day: Evening
4. Governing Planet: Mars
5. Angels: Seraphim
6. Chakras: Crown
7. Precious Stones: Amber
8. Tarot Card: Five of Pentacles
9. Candles: Black
10. Oils: Galangal Oil, Guinea Pepper Oil
11. Herbs: Cruel Man in the Woods, Mustard Seed, and Poke Root
12. Trees: Cherry tree
13. Animal presence: Raven, Insects

THE SPELL

On the night of a full moon take an egg make a small hole empty its contents and refill with guinea pepper oil, galangal oil and poke root and mustard seed. Then place on a bed of cruel man in the woods where the enemy will find it.

INTENTION: CAUSE MENTAL DISTURBANCE

1. Moon Phase: Waxing Moon
2. Day of the week: Thursday
3. Time of day: Evening
4. Governing Planet: Jupiter
5. Angels: Seraphim
6. Chakras: Crown
7. Precious Stones: Amber
8. Tarot Card: Ace of Swords turned upside down
9. Candles: Black
10. Oils: Guinea Pepper Oil, capsicum Oil
11. Herbs: Tormentilla, Valerian, Nightshade, and Red Pepper
12. Trees: Cypress
13. Animal presence: Dragon Fly

THE SPELL

On a waxing moon after midday light a black candle with their name etched into it dressed with capsicum oil and nightshade then place a mixture of tormentila, tila and poke root along their path where the will walk over it, mental disturbance will soon follow.

INTENTION: CAUSE DEPRESSION

1. Moon Phase: Full Moon
2. Day of the week: Thursday
3. Time of day: Evening
4. Governing Planet: Jupiter
5. Angels: Seraphim
6. Chakras: Crown
7. Precious Stones: Obsidian
8. Tarot Card: Two of Cups turned upside down
9. Candles: Black
10. Oils: Guinea Pepper Oil, Vertivert Oil
11. Herbs: Tilia, Tormentilla and Valerian
12. Trees: Cypress Tree
13. Animal presence: Dragon Fly

THE SPELL

On the night of a full moon take a doll to represent the enemy sprinkle with tormentila, tila and valerian. Take a pin and puncture the head of the doll and leave it there, now cover with a black cloth and bury it.

INTENTION: CAUSE MISUNDERSTANDING

1. Moon Phase: Full Moon
2. Day of the week: Wednesday
3. Time of day: Evening
4. Governing Planet: Mercury
5. Angels: Seraphim
6. Chakras: Crown
7. Precious Stones: Amber
8. Tarot Card: Two of Swords turned upside down
9. Candles: Black
10. Oils: Red Pepper Oil, Guinea Pepper Oil
11. Herbs: Twitch's Grass, Lemon Verbena, and Black Mustard seed
12. Trees: Cypress
13. Animal presence: Skunks, Bats

THE SPELL

On a full moon light a black candle dressed in red pepper oil, as you invoke the presence of a skunk. Then sprinkle twitch's grass, lemon verbena and black mustard seeds on the front door of their home.

INTENTION: CAUSE DEATH

1. Moon Phase: Full Moon
2. Day of the week: Saturday
3. Time of day: Midnight
4. Governing Planet: Saturn
5. Angels: Seraphim
6. Chakras: Crown
7. Precious Stones: Cinnabar
8. Tarot Card: Death Card
9. Candles: Black
10. Oils: Red Pepper Oil, Vandal Oil
11. Herbs: Wormwood, Colchicum, Henbane, Bat Nut, Acacia Leaf
12. Trees: Cherry Tree
13. Animal presence: Raven

THE SPELL

On the night of a full moon light a black candle dressed in vandal oil and red candle dressed in red pepper oil, light the black candle first place it on the left side place the red on the right side. Between the candles sprinkle a wormwood colchium and henbane place the death card above the herbs. On parchment paper in dragons blood write the Christian name of the enemy backwards. Add one of their socks or shoes envision the raven destroying your enemy, then take the sock or shoe with the herbs parchment paper and place it in a small box to bury at midnight near their home.

INTENTION: BECOME A DARK ANGEL

1. Moon Phase: Full Moon
2. Day of the week: Saturday
3. Time of day: Midnight
4. Governing Planet: Saturn
5. Angels: Seraphim
6. Chakras: Crown
7. Precious Stones: Cinnabar, Carnelian
8. Tarot Card: Chariot
9. Candles: Black
10. Oils: Patchouli, Asafoetida
11. Herbs: Willow, Wormwood, Valerian Root
12. Trees: Cypress
13. Animal presence: Raven

THE SPELL

On the night of a full moon, as you light a black candle, see a raven in your minds eye. Now dress the candle with willow. Take a black container add nine patchouli drops, some wormwood and valerian root inside the container then add three drops of asofoetida and smear it on the outside of the black container. Next go inside the nearest cemetery grab a small amount of graveyard dirt and place it in the black container and take it with you, as you leave the cemetery you will gain your dark wings and become a dark angel.

INTENTION: INVOKE DEMONS

1. Moon Phase: Full Moon
2. Day of the week: Saturday
3. Time of day: Midnight
4. Governing Planet: Saturn
5. Angels: Seraphim
6. Chakras: Crown
7. Precious Stones: Bloodstone
8. Tarot Card: Temperance
9. Candles: Black
10. Oils: Vervain oil
11. Herbs: Willow, Bat Nut, Mullein
12. Trees: Cypress
13. Animal presence: Horned Owl, Raven

THE SPELL

On the night of a full moon at midnight light a black candle dressed with vervain oil. Draw a triangle on the ground and place the candle in the center of the triangle over a bed of willow and bat nut. Place a bloodstone on the tip of the triangle. Invoke the demons.

INTENTION: CALL THE DEVIL

1. Moon Phase: Full Moon
2. Day of the week: Saturday
3. Time of day: Midnight
4. Governing Planet: Saturn
5. Angels: Seraphim
6. Chakras: Crown
7. Precious Stones: Cinnabar, carnelian
8. Tarot Card: Fool
9. Candles: Black
10. Oils: Sulphur, Asafoetida, and Patchouli
11. Herbs: Willow
12. Trees: Cypress
13. Animal presence: Raven, Horned Owl

THE SPELL

On the night of a full moon, at midnight in a secluded crossroads light a black candle dressed with asafetida, sulphur and patchouli. On your left hand hold a cinnabar stone and on your right hand a carnelian stone. At the crossroads directly underneath your feet sprinkle willow on the ground and stand over it as you envision a raven and call upon the devil, you will receive an immediate reply.

INTENTION: PACT WITH THE DEVIL

1. Moon Phase: Full Moon
2. Day of the week: Saturday
3. Time of day: Midnight
4. Governing Planet: Saturn
5. Angels: Seraphim
6. Chakras: Crown
7. Precious Stones: Carnelian, Cinnabar
8. Tarot Card: Hanged Man
9. Candles: Black
10. Oils: Vandal Root Oil, Patchouli Oil, and Frankincense
11. Herbs: Dragon Blood Root, Valerian Root, Willow
12. Trees: Cypress
13. Animal presence: Bats, Raven

THE SPELL

On the night of a full moon, at midnight in a secluded crossroads light a black candle dressed with vandal root oil, frankincense oil and patchouli oil. On virgin parchment paper write 666 with dragon blood directly underneath write your name then below your name write the word eternity. At the center of the crossroads sprinkle valerian root, willow and cypress then stand above it. On your left side place a cinnabar stone and on your right side a carnelian stone. Envision a bat in your minds eye call upon the devil, your pact is complete you will receive a sign.

INTENTION: EXORCISM

1. Moon Phase: Waning Moon
2. Day of the week: Saturday
3. Time of day: Midday
4. Governing Planet: Saturn
5. Angels: Michael
6. Chakras: Crown
7. Precious Stones: Diamond
8. Tarot Card: World Card
9. Candles: White
10. Oils: Holy Saint oil
11. Herbs: Wormwood, Blackberry leaf, pine needles
12. Trees: Ash
13. Animal presence: Horned Owl, Bald Eagle

THE SPELL

On a waning moon, light a large white candle and dress it with holy saint oil and sprinkle it with bayberry leafs on the right side of the candle place the world card. Place salt and pine needles on the entire floor of the area needing to be cleansed and leave it there for one night the next morning remove the salt. Then envision the horned owl as you place salt and pine needles around the perimeter of your home or place leaving it to dissipate on its own the exorcism is done.

INTENTION: CAST OUT DEMONS

1. Moon Phase: Full Moon
2. Day of the week: Saturday
3. Time of day: Midday
4. Governing Planet: Saturn
5. Angels: Michael
6. Chakras: Crown
7. Precious Stones: Diamond, Crystal
8. Tarot Card: Devil turned upside down
9. Candles: White
10. Oils: Holy Saint Oil
11. Herbs: Sacred Bark, Wormwood, and Yerba Santa
12. Trees: Ash
13. Animal presence: Red Tail Hawks, Spiders

THE SPELL

On a full moon cast a talcum powder circle on the floor where you stand for protection, light twelve small candles dressed in holy saint oil sprinkled with sacred bark, yerba santa lay over the herbs, the card of the devil turned upside down hold in your right hand a crystal. Envision a white light around you as the spirit of the angel Michael embraces you. Call upon the presence of the red tail hawk and from the circle throw ash tree leaves on the floor around you outside of the circle and say to ashes you return. The demons will be cast out immediately.

EPILOGUE

The war between black and white, good and evil has raged on for millenniums. It is said that evil governs the physical plane while good governs the ethereal spiritual plane. The good is the ideal state of human behavior. Spell casting evolved as an alternative energy a method of obtaining one's desired results. Spell casting foundation is magic whether its white or black magic.

The majority of life's experiences can be best served with the use of white magic spells. This book fully expresses white and black magic spell casting in its full glory, the two paths have been laid out, the path you take is up to you. In this book you will find spells for the majority of life's experiences and human desires. Whatever side of magic you practice it's important to be open-minded and to have respect for the beliefs and practices of those with opposing opinions. Always remember that contrast and differences are the seeds of creation. Spell casting can better your life, eliminate issues, bring fourth wealth and allow you to heal yourself and others. Never cast a spell for someone unless they have requested it and only the form of magic that appeals to you or calls you. White magic is used for benevolent reasons summoning the elements and light. While black magic is intended for dark purposes that can be seen as evil that can cause harm to enemies while destroying their wellbeing. Black magic has the power to reverse our fate receiving redemption from apparent failures. The super natural powers of the underworld are not bound by law they simply wait to be summoned to then use their intervening powers to bring fourth your desires. To be effective black magic requires of you full loyalty and worship. Black and white magic have always coexisted side by side very much like North and South being at opposite poles.

    White magic is based on respect, love and light. White spell casting is used for manifestation as it sends out into the universe a direct request of your desires. White spell casting opens a path for manifestation through conjuring a specific spell to bring good into your life. White magic simply allows us to focus and direct our intention by setting the appropriate spell and visualizing the end result. White spell casting assists us by adding positive elements directed at a desire. Through spells we attract blessings by anointing essential elements in our rituals. Therefore white spell casting is considered to be a positive form of spell casting whereas black magic is seen as a negative unnatural process used to achieve desired results.

www.ingramcontent.com/pod-product-compliance
Lightning Source LLC
Chambersburg PA
CBHW070641050426
42451CB00008B/260